# FUTUREPROOFED: CRAFTING YOUR RETIREMENT IN THE AI ERA

Hayden Van Der Post

**Reactive Publishing**

*To my daughter, may she know anything is possible.*

# CONTENTS

# INTRODUCTION

## *The traditional retirement paradigm vs. the modern shift*

The idea of retirement and what it entails has undergone significant shifts over the past few decades. The traditional paradigm of retirement paints an image of rest and relaxation, a well-deserved break after years of hard work. It is commonly perceived as the stage of life where one completely stops working and devotes their time to pursuing passions, spending time with loved ones, and maximizing leisure activities.

Yet, in the context of the modern era, this traditional view of retirement seems almost archaic. Technological advancements, societal shifts, changes in the global job market and longer life expectancy have transformed the dynamics of retirement to a great extent. The linear life cycle of education, employment, and retirement is no longer the only viable path.

This dramatic shift has induced a reimagination of retirement, which is now seen less as a full stop and more as a pivot or a transition phase. Today, it's not uncommon for retirees to take on part-time jobs, consulting roles, or even start new businesses entirely. The sharp divide between work life and retirement has blurred, giving rise to various new retirement models.

Moreover, in modern retirement, ongoing education has become critically important. With the pace of technological change, professionals across all fields are pushed to continuously learn and adapt. This is equally true for retirees who choose to remain in the workforce in some capacity. Additionally, this idea of continuous learning also extends beyond one's professional life. The promotion of brain health and cognitive vitality through intellectually stimulating activities is an emerging trend in retirement planning.

It is also worth noting how the perception of age itself has changed in the modern era. The old adage 'age is just a number' has never been truer. Today, turning 60 or 65 doesn't automatically render someone too old to work or contribute. This change in societal attitudes has contributed to the rising trend of delayed retirement.

On a more challenging note, the modern era has brought about its own set of financial complications that retirees need to navigate. The shift away from traditional pension schemes, the unpredictability of markets, and the increased cost of living make today retirement planning a complex puzzle to solve. It requires robust financial strategies, risk management, and in many cases, the ability to generate income post-retirement.

While the essence of retirement remains consistent — to have the freedom to enjoy the fruits of one’s labour— the ways in which these manifests are vastly diverse and evolving. The new retirement paradigm demands adaptability, lifelong learning, financial astuteness, and a willingness to redefine traditional aging norms. Ultimately, the aim is to create a fulfilling and financially secure retirement that aligns with an individual's unique goals, lifestyle preferences, and values.

## The changing face of retirement in the modern era

There are many factors influencing retirement perspectives today. Some of these trends are age-old factors that have always been a part of retirement planning, but have taken on new significance due to the rapidly changing landscape. Simultaneously, we're seeing the emergence of entirely new considerations brought about by shifts in technology, economic structures, and societal values.

One of the most significant factors influencing retirement perspectives is the changing demographics of age and life. As we see impressive strides in healthcare and wellness, people are living longer than ever before. For many, reaching the ages of 60 or 65 no longer signifies the end of work life, but a transition into new opportunities and challenges. In fact, many choose to continue working beyond the traditional retirement age, either due to financial necessity or personal fulfillment, drastically transforming the retirement landscape.

Additionally, the evolving nature of work significantly impacts retirement perspectives. Introduction of Artificial Intelligence and automation into the workforce has led to considerable anxiety around job security, particularly among older adults. However, it's not all doom and gloom. AI also presents opportunities for new kinds of work and has the potential to make work less physically demanding, which could be a boon for an ageing workforce. In this context, the phenomenon of the gig economy also plays a crucial role. It provides flexibility, allows people to work less than full-time, and even lets people continue to work into old age without the pressure of a traditional 9-to-5 job.

The modern economy with its unique challenges and

opportunities also shapes retirement perspectives. Increased life expectancy combined with leaner pension funds and potential economic instability means people need to think more critically about their finances. They now have to consider how they can ensure their savings last longer while still meeting their retirement lifestyle goals. This factor has given rise to more sophisticated financial planning strategies and has made financial literacy a crucial skill for upcoming retirees.

The influence of societal and cultural changes cannot be underplayed when discussing shifts in retirement perspectives. The societal view towards work and retirement forms an important backdrop to the way individuals envision their own retirement. With the societal view towards age and productivity becoming more flexible, we are seeing a less rigid approach to retirement, one that values continuous contribution, learning, and adaptation.

Lastly, embracing technology's role in our lives also affects our retirement perspectives. Technology is not just changing the way we work but also the way we plan for and live in retirement. With everything from AI-driven investment platforms to digital healthcare and networking platforms, technology is making it possible for retirees to stay financially secure, healthy, connected, and occupied during their retirement years.

When we factor in all these shifts, it is clear that retirement today is a far more dynamic concept than it has ever been. The key to navigating these changes is adaptability and a willingness to break from traditional norms. It's about envisioning retirement not as the end of something but as the opportunity for new beginnings. And these beginnings are influenced significantly by our changing perspectives on age, work, financial security, societal norms, and of course, technology.

## The changing face of retirement in the modern era

Stepping into the 21st century, we were welcomed by a technology-driven era – one that has revolutionized every facet of our lives from the way we work, communicate, entertain ourselves to how we plan for the future. Primarily, when it comes to retirement planning, technology not only holds the power of making everything more efficient and precise but also brings forth a set of implications.

As we stand on the brink of a new AI era, it warrants a profound exploration into the consequential role that technology is playing in altering our lives, careers and ultimately our retirement.

At the forefront of this technological revolution, Artificial Intelligence (AI) and automation stand as game-changers. AI continued to make headlines throughout the last decade, not just as a futuristic concept or a millennial trend, but as a revolutionary technology that could substantially alter the job market. Automation, coupled with AI, presents a significant risk to job sectors bound around redundant and replicable tasks, pushing individuals towards the dire need for upskilling and enhancing their skillsets in tune with the evolving job market.

Further amplifying these shifts is the rise of the gig economy. Powered by technological advancements, freelancing platforms have sprouted all over the internet, creating an array of opportunities for those looking for more control over their work schedules. This has been particularly beneficial for people on the brink of retirement or already retired who are looking to supplement their income.

Beyond job markets, AI's influence transcends to the realm of financial planning and wealth management, key components of retirement planning. Personal Financial Management (PFM) tools powered by AI algorithms can help individuals track their expenses, optimize savings, and make well-informed investment decisions. Robo-advisors have made it easier for individuals to manage their investments, utilizing advanced algorithms to provide financial advice and digital investment management with minimal human intervention.

Technology is also impacting the healthcare industry, which in turn, affects retirement planning. Digital healthcare advancements like telemedicine, AI-powered diagnosis, wearable health monitors, and virtual reality therapeutics are radically transforming healthcare services, enabling a longer, healthier life, and thereby affecting the period of retirement and the potential healthcare costs during retirement.

Despite the multitude of ways technology aids in retirement planning, it also brings along a new set of challenges. Issues like cybersecurity, privacy threats, fear of technology, and increased reliance on these digital platforms are critical to consider as we delegate more of our life's decisions to technology. Furthermore, with increasing AI capabilities, a thorough understanding of how these AI systems work becomes paramount to avoid unfair practices due to inherent biases in their functioning.

The role of technology, particularly AI, is pivotal in shaping retirement in the modern era. It brings forth new opportunities for managing work-life, finances, and health, but also presses us to adapt and evolve continuously to leverage the best of these advancements and mitigate the subsequent challenges. As we move forward, the ability to navigate the technological landscape will prove to be an essential asset for a secure and fulfilling retirement future.

# THE IMPACT OF TECHNOLOGICAL ADVANCEMENTS ON OUR FUTURE

## *Overview of major tech shifts in the last two decades*

The rapidly evolving landscape of technology has made its presence felt in every aspect of life, including the way we plan for our retirement. Over the last two decades, we have borne witness to many substantial tech shifts that have altered our relationship with the world and redefined our life experiences. Let's take a deep dive into these major technological transformations and their implications.

As we thread the path back to the late 20th century, the broad tapestry of technology evolution unveils itself. It introduces us to the dawn of the internet, which promised a connected world, but the reality of its vast potential was yet to be fully comprehended.

Heading into the 2000s, with the internet spreading its roots deeper into our lives, we experienced the dot-com bubble, an era of excessive speculation and escalated market valuations of tech-oriented companies. The bubble later burst, leading to crashed stocks and vanished fortunes, but it laid the groundwork for futuristic internet-based business models.

If the 2000s was a testament to the power of the internet, the ensuing decade amplified this by ushering in the age of Social Media. Platforms like Facebook, Twitter, LinkedIn and the likes gave a new definition to global connectivity and communication. It reshaped human relations, creating a parallel digital world where people converged, interacted, and even carried out business deals. For retirees, social media presented a novel way to stay in touch with society, engage in discussions, and even explore new economic opportunities.

Parallely, the trajectory of technological growth was being charted on another frontier – smartphones. Apple's entry into the market with iPhone in 2007 marked a significant transition. Smartphones became an extension of our selves. They provided access to a multitude of tools - from health monitoring to investment tracking - that could assist with a retiree's day-to-day management tasks.

The most recent phase of tech shifts is marked by the emergence of the digital economy or the gig economy. Platforms like Uber, Airbnb, and Freelancer.com have made it easier for people to monetize their assets, skills, and time. This development is of particular importance when we talk about retirement, as it creates an environment that allows for flexible working arrangements even past retirement age.

Among all of these innovations, the one innovation that has been subtly weaving itself into all these developments, backing them, and driving them forward, is Artificial Intelligence. From

Siri on your iPhones to algorithm-driven financial advice, AI has been seamlessly integrated into various aspects of our lives. Today, AI is poised not just to aid human efforts but to potentially automate them, a prospect that holds varied implications for the current and future workforce.

Delving deeper into the 21st century, we are introduced to a world that not only holds promises of further tech revolutions, especially in the domain of AI, but also poses challenges and uncertainties. As valuable as these tech shifts are, they require us to continuously adapt and update ourselves to remain relevant and prepared - an essential attribute for a secure and fulfilling retirement in this digital age.

**Predicted Technological Trajectories for the Next 20 Years**

Peering into the crystal ball of technological development for the next 20 years, we're presented with a future equally exciting and disruptive. This forecasted landscape predominantly revolves around automation, data, and artificial intelligence.

Automation and Robotics have been brewing around for some time now but are expected to take centre stage in the coming decades. More and more industries are looking to minimize human involvement in repetitive and hazardous tasks by integrating automation technologies into their operations.

Entire industries, from manufacturing to agriculture, are predicted to witness a new level of efficiency and productivity, redefining labor economics. While this translates to an improved standard of living, it also engenders a potential dislocation of traditional jobs. As retirees or prospective retirees, it presents a dual challenge - adapting to a world increasingly managed by machines and reinventing oneself in an evolving job market.

Another burgeoning trajectory is that of big data and analytics. The exponential growth of data generation and collection has given rise to the era of big data. The ability to process this data efficiently and draw intelligent insights from it paves the way for data analysis jobs, a growing field with excellent demand. From predicting market trends to personalizing product recommendations, data analytics is being integrated into every aspect of business. This is a realm of technology where retirees can pivot, leveraging their wealth of experience and domain knowledge, aided by requisite upskilling.

Finally, Artificial Intelligence and Machine Learning will continue their upward trend, cutting across multiple sectors and permeating deeper into our daily routines. As AI technology improves, we can expect advances in predictive algorithms, decision-making capabilities, and personalization.

Looking specifically at the financial sector, AI has the potential to revolutionize how we manage our finances and plan for retirement. AI-powered robo-advisors could offer personalized investment advice, automated budgeting tools that help manage everyday expenses, and predictive models that provide a glimpse into potential financial outcomes.

For retirees, this level of personalization could mean more accurate financial advice and guidance tailored to individual financial goals and risk tolerance levels. With AI continually learning and improving from vast amounts of financial data, the potential for error reduces, making for a more reliable and efficient retirement planning process.

Healthcare, an integral consideration area for retirees, won't be left untouched either. AI in conjunction with big data can lead to personalized healthcare plans, early disease detection, accurate diagnostics, and advanced treatment options.

What ties all these technological trajectories together is the pervasive Internet of Things (IoT). As more devices become interconnected, vast amounts of user data become available. This data drives insights used in AI models, leading to more efficient systems and personalized user experiences.

However, alongside the immense opportunities, these technological advances also present challenges. From job displacement due to automation to privacy concerns arising from extensive data collection, it's important to navigate these waters carefully. Providing security in this technology-laden future will be a key pillar of consideration for retirement planning.

As we stand on the precipice of these striking advancements, the key takeaway is that retirees need to build adaptability into their plans. Continued learning and staying abreast with emerging technologies becomes not just a good-to-do, but a necessary strategy to navigate and flourish in the AI-driven era.

In summary, this grand reveal of technology paints a picture of a future where AI plays a central role, reshaping industries, affecting labor markets, and redefining societal norms. As we step into this future, it is crucial to understand these trends and what they mean for retirement planning, placing us in the driver's seat of our future.

## How These Tech Changes Redefine Retirement Planning

Technology, especially the advent of AI, is not only transforming our everyday lives and work environments but is becoming increasingly entwined with our long-term financial and retirement planning. This chapter aims to shed light on just how these tech advancements endorse a reimagined approach to retirement.

Firstly, employment paradigms are shifting with the advancement of automation and AI technologies. We are transitioning from a labor market defined by full-time employment to one more inclined towards gig-based, freelance, and part-time work. This shift brings about changes in the income steadiness, retirement savings, and financial security of individuals. It demands a more dynamic and flexible approach, championing multiple income streams and a diversified investment portfolio as means to ensure sustained income post-retirement. Tech companies, for instance, Airbnb or Uber, are presenting older adults with opportunities to tap into these emerging markets, augmenting their financial stability.

Secondly, technological sophistication in healthcare could significantly enhance the quality and longevity of life. Wearable technology, personalized healthcare, data-driven diagnostics, and telemedicine are not just buzzwords but show a clear path toward a future where quality healthcare is both more accessible and affordable. Retirees stand to benefit significantly from these advancements, potentially facing lower healthcare costs and improved health, which will further impact their financial calculations for retirement.

Concurrently, the rise of AI in financial planning cannot be understated. The integration of AI into financial services is simplifying finance and making it more accessible. Robo-advisors, for example, use algorithms to analyze your financial position, risk tolerance, and long-term goals to provide personalized investment advice. This not only democratizes access to high-quality financial advice but offers a level of precision that human advisors might not achieve consistently. Tools like these can provide more reliable forecasts of retirement savings growth and expenditure trends, contributing to more accurate and tailored retirement strategies.

AI algorithms can also assist in budgeting, detecting potentially fraudulent activity, and offer suggestions for tax savings - all important considerations for strengthening financial security in retirement. Additionally, the automation of various financial operations could reduce the chances of human error, leading to more efficient retirement fund management.

In a landscape where AI is also being leveraged to predict future market trends, retirees can be better equipped to deal with the vagaries of markets through AI-driven investment strategies. Whether it be conventional stock markets or newer domains like cryptocurrencies, AI has the potential to alleviate some of the unpredictabilities that come with investment decisions.

While these technological trends bring along a new dawn of opportunities, they also ring in a set of challenges. Automation risks job displacement, and data-driven technologies pose significant questions about data privacy and security. Preparing for these new risks necessitates a reevaluation of insurance, personal data protection measures, and plans for potential periods of unemployment or career shifting.

The essence, thus, points to a retirement planning framework that is more comprehensive and forward-looking than ever before. The key to navigating this terrain lies in understanding these tech trends and adapting accordingly, both in terms of financial and lifestyle choices. The involvement of learnership, adaptability, and technological acceptance can indeed empower the populace to carve out retirements that are not only financially secure but also enriched with purpose and possibility.

Change is the only constant, as they say, and in the case of retirement planning, the winds of change are blowing heavily in the favour of technology. Understanding and embracing these technological shifts is not merely an option, but a crucial necessity for those aiming to retire gracefully into a future shaped increasingly by AI.

# CHAPTER 1: THE EVOLUTION OF RETIREMENT

# A BRIEF HISTORY OF RETIREMENT

## *Origins and Cultural Differences in Retirement Concepts*

Understanding retirement requires us to immerse ourselves in its historical context and the cultural nuances that define it. Traditional notions of retirement have evolved remarkably over time and vary broadly across different cultures, affecting how societies perceive it.

The concept of retirement is quite modern, with its etymological roots in the French word 'retraite,' which means 'withdrawal' or 'retreat.' It is worth noting that such an idea was absent in ancient societies, where people generally worked till the end of their lives to sustain themselves and their families. There was no pre-defined age that signaled the end of a person's productive years.

The first formal pension systems, precursors to modern retirement, emerged in the late 19th century. In 1889, German Chancellor Otto von Bismarck instituted the first social insurance program, providing income to those above 70 who were no longer able to work. Notably, this age was chosen because few people lived past it, hinting at the expectation that people were to work until they could not.

In the United States, the Social Security Act of 1935 set the retirement age at 65, effectively institutionalizing the concept of retirement. Coupled with the rise of private pension schemes offered by employers throughout the 20th century, retirement gradually became an expected life stage rather than an option for a select few.

However, perceptions of retirement vary dramatically across different cultures worldwide. For instance, traditional Confucian principles revered in East Asian societies prize age and seniority, seeing older individuals as wise sources of guidance rather than as non-contributors. Such societies emphasize intergenerational cohabitation, with adult children often taking responsibility for their parents' care, reducing the need for a robust retirement scheme.

In contrast, the Scandinavian nations' welfare model promotes the notion of a 'positive retirement,' wherein retirement is not a sign of social exclusion but indicates decent living standards, adequate pensions, and a healthy, enjoyable post-work life. Here, the retirement age often correlates with the quality of the healthcare system and the robustness of the welfare state.

In some cultures, retirement is more a gradient than a binary switch from working to not working. For example, certain Native American tribes encourage older adults to gradually reduce their workload while increasingly becoming custodians of cultural knowledge and traditions.

What's clear, however, is that broad shifts in demographics and technology are creating a global convergence towards redefining retirement. Longer life expectancies, courtesy of advances in healthcare, are pushing the retirement age higher in many societies. Concurrently, societal reliance on technology and automation is phasing out certain job roles traditionally held by older workers, adding a layer of complexity to the retirement equation.

In light of this, it becomes critical to understand the various dimensions shaping retirement across cultures and eras. As we shift to an AI-driven world where human longevity reaches unprecedented levels, the need to design sustainable, flexible retirement paradigms that reconcile cultural, economic, and technological transitions is more urgent than ever. It's time to reimagine retirement - not as a uniform, one-size-fits-all concept, but as a dynamic, culturally nuanced, and richly varied life stage.

**The Rise and Transformation of Pension Systems**

The concept of a pension system, while not entirely novel, has experienced significant transformations since its early inception. Tracing the eddies of change in pension systems throughout history provides a valuable backdrop against which to view forecasted AI-induced developments.

Our foray into the history of pensions starts in the ancient world. In Rome around 13 B.C, Augustus, the first Roman Emperor, introduced 'annona civica,' an annual grain allowance given to citizens who could not work. Despite its rudimentary nature, this provision marked one of the earliest instances of social security.

The first semblance of the modern pension system, however, originates in the late 19th century from Germany. As part of sweeping socialist reforms, German Chancellor Otto von Bismarck instituted a state-supported social insurance program in 1889. It officialized a retirement age (70), promising a pension to those no longer able to work.

A few decades later, the United States institutionalized retirement through the 1935 Social Security Act. It introduced a federal safety net for the elderly, the unemployed, and the disadvantaged. The retirement age was set at 65, closely following Bismarck's model. Simultaneously, private companies began offering pension plans to employees, promoting loyalty and long-term service.

Post-World War II, during the mid-20th century, the 'Golden Age of Capitalism' saw the promotion of 'Defined Benefit' pensions. These guaranteed employees a specific payout upon retirement, calculated on length of service and salary. This type of system underpinned the comforting ideal of a loyal, lifelong employee rewarded with a worry-free retirement.

However, the economic volatility of the 1970s and 80s forced a transition towards 'Defined Contribution' pension plans. Unlike their predecessors, these plans did not guarantee a specific payout but depended on the individual's (and employer's) contributions and the returns from investing these funds. This system transfered investment risk from the employer to the employee, with the retiree's financial security tied closely to market performance.

A significant shift coinciding with this change was a broad move towards 'individual responsibility' for retirement savings, exemplified by increased promotion of private savings accounts and Individual Retirement Accounts (IRAs). The late 20th century was undoubtedly marked by the surge in 401(k) plans in the U.S and similar structures worldwide.

In recent years, governments' and employers' role in retirement provision is decreasing, exacerbated by an aging demographic and increasing longevity. The 'three-pillar' system, proposed by the World Bank in 1994, has been widely accepted, encompassing: a publicly managed, tax-financed social safety net; a mandatory private pension; and voluntary personal savings or insurance.

However, the financial crisis of 2008, revealing the vulnerabilities of a market-dependent pension system, sparked debates about revising the current pension scheme. Indeed, the stress-train is visible, with underfunded pension liabilities being a significant concern for both public and corporations alike.

Presently, we stand on the brink of another transformation. With the advent of artificial intelligence and increasing life expectancy, traditional pension systems' adequacy and sustainability are under scrutiny. Adapting to these changes by crafting a retirement system that meshes security with flexibility is the new challenge for modern societies.

In the face of uncertain times, heightened by unpredictable tech advancements, one thing is clear: navigating the future of retirement will require not just individual adaptability, but also systemic resilience and reconfiguration. This tome intends to educate, guide, and provoke thought about how best to tackle the challenges and opportunities heading our way, ensuring a future where retirement is not just financially secure, but also smoothly tailored to individuals' changing needs in an AI-driven world.

## The Relationship Between Work, Age, and Societal Value

When considering retirement and its intricacies, one cannot extricate the narrative from the crucial triad of work, age, and societal value. Understanding this relationship is vital to fully appreciate retirement's shifting landscape, particularly in the face of artificial intelligence transformation.

The evolution of societies across the world has witnessed a continual redefinition of 'work'. Ancient civilizations often incorporated all stages of a person's life into a cohesive community function. The stratification of labor based on age was relatively unclear, and work was less a profession than an integral part of survival and community life.

During the Industrial Revolution, a significant bifurcation occurred, segregating work from home and leisure. 'Work' became a paid occupation, taking place outside the domestic boundaries. Factory environments demanded physical strength, favoring younger individuals and redefining the life stages: childhood, work years, and old-age. With diminished strength and increased susceptibility to sickness or injuries, the elderly gradually retired from the workforce.

This was the genesis of 'retirement'. The concept hinged on replacing older, potentially less productive workers with younger, more robust counterparts, heavily tethering societal value to economic productivity. Thus, ‘retirement’ carried a societal message: after a specific age, one's productivity is expected to drop. Consequently, there arose the concept of 'mandatory retirement age,' aligning older adults' societal contribution or 'value' to their workforce participation.

However, the 20th century heralded changes in this perspective. Increasing life expectancy, better healthcare, and shifting societal priorities undoubtedly played roles in this transition.

A notable paradigm shift has recognized older adults as productive contributors, no longer exclusively tied to their economic output.

For example, many developed countries, witnessing talent shortages, began encouraging older adults to stay engaged in the workforce. Some workforce sectors, such as consulting or academia, appreciate the value of experience and wisdom that older employees provide. Furthermore, societal value is now also associated with generous volunteer activities post-retirement, community engagements, and even the opportunity to explore new hobbies and interests.

Unfortunately, ageism still persists, often stripping away the perceived societal value of our more experienced population sector. There is a need to keep challenging the stereotype that equates 'value' exclusively to 'productivity'. Instead, framing societal worth as multifaceted, combining wisdom, experience, individuality, interpersonal relationships, and personal growth, is vitally important.

In the AI era, this issue has grown more significant. As artificial intelligence has started to disrupt traditional workforce structures, we face new potentials and challenges. For example, automation threatens job roles across all age groups, which requires us to reassess value distribution across different ages and occupations.

However, AI also opens up opportunities for older adults. Intelligent systems could automate physically demanding tasks, enabling older adults to remain productive longer. AI can also provide platforms for mentorship, allowing retired professionals to pass on their wisdom to younger generations.

Thus, in the AI era, the relationship between work, age, and societal value becomes more complex and nuanced, necessitating our deeper understanding and mindfulness in crafting retirement systems.

In our path forward, we must look back at our shared human history, understand the lessons it offers, and deftly weave those lessons into a new narrative — one that positions retirement not as the closing of a chapter, but rather the exciting commencement of a new one. A narrative where age doesn't equate to obsoleteness, but oozes wisdom, an opportunity for personal growth, community contribution, and varied forms of societal value that extend well beyond pure economic productivity.

# HOW AI AND AUTOMATION ARE RESHAPING WORK AND LIFE

## *Case Studies of Industries Disrupted by AI*

Artificial Intelligence has undoubtedly become an influential player in the global business landscape, effectuating a paradigmatic shift in varied sectors. In understanding the AI-centric challenges and possibilities for retirement, it is insightful to hone in on industries already disrupted by AI. Below, we delve into three salient case studies underlining AI's transformative impact on the healthcare, financial services, and retail sectors.

AI and Healthcare: A Flourishing Symbiotic Relationship

Healthcare, a cornerstone of our society, has witnessed revolutionary changes precipitated by AI. These advancements have optimised the functioning of the sector, ensuring efficient diagnostic, therapeutic, and preventive measures, thus contributing to increased life expectancy.

An illustration of this change can be found in the onset of AI in the field of radiology. Deep-learning algorithms have become exceptionally proficient at identifying pathologies in medical images, matching or even surpassing human counterparts in speed and accuracy. 'Zebra Medical Vision,' a medical imaging start-up, implements AI to scan imaging records for early detection of diseases like lung cancer, cardiovascular conditions, and liver diseases.

In AI's therapeutic applications, 'Optellum', a lung health medtech startup, developed a 'Virtual Nodule Clinic' capable of diagnosing lung cancer much earlier than traditional procedures. Also, IBM's Watson for Oncology helps doctors create personalized cancer treatment plans. Their AI offers informed recommendations by comparing patient information to previous similar cases and the latest medical research.

AI's Preventive Health features empowering people to become active participants in their health have enormous implications on retirement, with potential to transform the way we age.

AI Revolution in Financial Services

AI has been instrumental in reshaping global financial services. From customer service chatbots to AI-driven investment advice, financial institutions are swiftly integrating AI into their core businesses.

Robo-advisors such as 'Betterment' and 'Wealthfront' use AI to offer personalized financial advice and portfolio management services, significantly lowering the bar for entry into the world of investing.

Meanwhile, AI in fraud detection has enhanced security in digital transactions. Companies like 'Mastercard' leverage AI to analyse millions of transactions per minute, detecting suspicious activities, thereby ensuring a secure digital economy.

AI's influence in managing personal finances and ensuring transactional security equips retirees with tools fostering financial independence in a secure digital realm.

AI's Retail Renaissance

The retail sector is undergoing an AI-driven Renaissance, enhancing personalized shopping experiences, inventory management, and trend prediction. AI has transformed retail into a data-driven industry optimizing profits and customer satisfaction.

'Amazon Go' stores epitomize this revolution. These AI-powered physical stores offer a checkout-free shopping experience. The system utilizes computer vision, deep learning algorithms, and sensor fusion, matching online convenience with a tangible in-store experience.

Clothing retailer 'Stitch Fix' takes personalization up a notch, leveraging AI to offer personalized style recommendations. Their algorithms blend personal style, size preference, and trends to deliver personalized clothing boxes—delivering a unique customer experience.

The data-driven nature of AI in retail has led to highly personalized interactions, subsequently influencing customer behavior—a crucial consideration when strategizing ways to market the AI era's retirement tools and solutions.

Each of these sectors offers lessons on AI's ability to disrupt status quo, drive efficiencies, personalise services, and create altogether new paradigms. As AI continues its relentless march, impacting industries far and wide, retirees will need to adapt and thrive amidst this sea change. The revolution is not on the horizon; it has arrived. Forging a seamless blend of this AI-induced seismic shift into our retirement narrative is not an option; it's a necessity. As we delve further into AI's nuances, let's prepare for a journey of disruptions, opportunities, and transformation that will redefine our retirement story.

**Potential Job Sectors at Risk in the Near Future**

As we explore artificial intelligence's awe-inspiring advancements and transformative capabilities, it is crucial to address the elephant in the room – the potential job displacement deemed to occur due to AI. Factors driving this include but are not limited to automation, machine learning efficiency, and the cost-saving allure for a variety of industries. This section provides a concise analysis of job sectors that could potentially face risk in the next few years and explores how they can adapt to this evolving landscape.

Automation and Manufacturing

First on the docket is Manufacturing, a sector that has been witnessing automation's impact for decades. As AI technologies and robotics become increasingly sophisticated, we can anticipate a significant transformative shift in production lines, assembly work and packaging. A McKinsey report suggests that by 2030, up to 20% of work activities could be automated, leading to potential job displacement.

While this paradigm shift may seem intimidating, it's vital to understand that automation will not eradicate jobs entirely but transform them. The imminent need in this sphere will be to identify the skills necessary for automation-adjacent roles and equip the workforce accordingly.

Transportation

The transportation sector is facing significant disruption due to the rise of autonomous vehicles. While this may take a few more years to come to full fruition due to regulatory hurdles and the complexities of real-world situations, the writing is on the wall. The trucking industry, taxi services, and public transportation could see a considerable reduction in the need for human drivers.

Again, this changing landscape doesn't spell doom but indicates a call for reskilling and reeducation. Understanding AI technology, troubleshooting automated systems, and fleet management are some potential areas for focus.

Retail and Service Industries

AI's compelling influence in retail, as exemplified with Amazon Go stores, suggests a prospective shift towards cashier-less shopping experiences. Similarly, food service outlets are exploring automation in food preparation and service, translating into potential job losses in these sectors.

However, here too, the focus on customer experience and personal interaction suggests a shift in roles rather than complete elimination. Skillsets focusing on managing AI systems, enhancing customer experience, and supervising automated processes will be in demand.

Administrative Roles

AI's proficiency at processing and analyzing large volumes of data puts administrative roles at a potential risk. Machine learning algorithms can perform tasks such as scheduling appointments, data entry, and basic bookkeeping more efficiently and with fewer errors, setting the stage for a new reality for administrative assistants.

However, this could free up personnel to tackle more complex tasks that require a human touch, such as strategy planning, team management, and dealing with nuanced communication.

While it's imperative to acknowledge the potential risks AI poses to specific sectors, it's equally important to view AI as a tool that can unlock latent human potential. The human ability to adapt, empathize, strategize and innovate could never be more paramount as we look towards a future sculpted by AI. The jobs of the future may indeed be radically different from what we perceive them to be today. Yet, by strategically honing our uniquely human qualities and embracing lifelong learning, we can ensure that we remain not just relevant, but indispensable, in this AI era.

## Embracing AI: Adapting and Upskilling for Modern Job Roles

The advent of AI, far from being the harbinger of joblessness as many fear, is a clarion call for adaptation and upskilling. While certain roles may become automated, a parallel paradigm emerges – one that iterates the need for uniquely human skills and encourages career metamorphosis. The most significant move towards surviving and thriving in this era of disruption is to embrace artificial intelligence, understand its intricacies, and prepare ourselves for the modern roles it spurs.

## Understanding Artificial Intelligence

The first step is mastering a foundational understanding of AI. This extends beyond the realm of sole IT professionals and into the wider mainstream workforces. It's imperative to grasp the basics of artificial intelligence, machine learning, and data analytics, irrespective of your industry. Numerous online platforms offer relatively easy-to-understand crash courses on the basics of AI and machine learning. These provide an ideal starting point, even for those without an IT background.

## Digital Literacy

Secondly, digital literacy has become a non-negotiable skill. An understanding of digital tools, platforms, and basic coding can put employees ahead in their fields. Coding skills, coupled with problem-solving and innovative thinking, pave the way for transformative solutions applicable to a myriad of industries. Trading manual dexterity for digital dexterity is a transformation that can future-proof careers.

## Cultivating Transferable Skills

While technical prowess is crucial, placing high premiums on transferable skills like problem-solving, creativity, and emotional intelligence will be key in an AI-driven future. These "soft skills" are inherently human strengths that are irreplaceable by AI. Emotional intelligence, leadership, adaptability, and creative problem-solving are facets that AI, with its binary logic, cannot yet fully embrace.

## Upskilling and Lifelong Learning

The World Economic Forum forecasts that by 2025, the fast-paced tech skills race could lead us to reskill more than half of all employees. As AI technology steadily progresses and redefines traditional jobs, it compels us to reconsider our skill sets. This is where the pivot towards lifelong learning becomes a significant aspect of career planning.

Industries and educational institutions must work in unison to create affordable, accessible upskilling programs tethered to market needs. Emphasizing reskilling within an organization's culture and linking it to career progression could also boost employee engagement and retention.

## AI-Empowered Roles

Finally, the rise of AI propels numerous tech-intensive roles to prominence. AI-based job roles aren't confined to AI programming or development. Consider the spectrum of AI specialties: data scientists who analyze and interpret complex digital data, AI ethicists who navigate the moral conundrums artificial intelligence presents, or AI law specialists dealing with the legal aspects of AI implementation.

Meanwhile, many non-tech roles evolve in response to AI's rise. For instance, human resource professionals may increasingly use AI for recruiting but must also manage AI ethics policies, restructure teams disrupted by AI, and draft strategies to manage an AI-integrated workforce.

In summary, the AI era doesn't herald the end of human work; instead, it flags the start of its most exciting chapter. Embracing

AI means understanding its potential and limits, upskilling to remain relevant and adapting to a landscape suffused with constant innovation. In this era, lifelong learning is the most potent weapon, and adaptability, the most valuable skill. Far from rendering us obsolete, AI can make us the best version of ourselves - professionally and personally. Let this realization form the foundation of our journey in the AI era.

# THE CHANGING DEMOGRAPHICS: LIVING LONGER AND RETIRING LATER

## *Advances in Healthcare Leading to Increased Life Expectancy*

For millennia, humans have striven to understand how the body works and how to beat the physical breakdown that inevitably accompanies aging. Historically, the quest for longevity seemed a formidable challenge. However, the last century has seen significant advances in healthcare that not only allowed humans to live longer lives but have also enhanced the quality of those added years.

The Intersection of Medicine and Technology

At the forefront of advancing lifespans today, we find the intersection of medicine and technology. The reason behind this profound change is twofold. One, there's been a decisive shift towards preventative care and personalized medicine, ushering in a new era of healthcare management. Two, technologies like artificial intelligence and Big Data analysis are instrumental in the progress of healthcare, not only to treat diseases but also to predict and prevent them.

Shift towards Preventative Care

Preventive healthcare, which focuses on prophylactic treatments, has emerged as a priority for medical professionals and researchers. Previously, medicine was typically reactive - patients sought help after symptoms manifested. Today, the focus has moved upstream toward disease prevention. This movement is underpinned by an understanding that preventing diseases before they occur reduces healthcare costs and improves patient outcomes.

Advancements in Genetics and Personalized Medicine

Genome sequencing has been a revolutionary door opener towards personalized medicine and a longer life span. The human genome project, for instance, has provided unprecedented insights into genetic predispositions for health conditions and potential responses to drugs. It paved the way for genetic testing, allowing individuals and doctors to monitor and understand an individual's genetic vulnerability to certain diseases. Consequently, treatments can be proactive and tailored to individuals, further increasing lifespans.

Artificial Intelligence in Healthcare

AI deployment in healthcare has similarly set historical milestones. Machine learning algorithms sifting through vast swathes of electronic health records can predict disease onset, helping doctors preemptively address health concerns. AI-powered devices are guiding health maintenance outside of clinical settings, allowing for remote patient monitoring, which enhances outpatient care and reduces strain on medical facilities.

Improvement in Sanitation and Immunization

Meanwhile, global efforts to improve sanitation and food supplies have decreased the incidence of communicable diseases, which were once primary mortality causes. Immunization campaigns, coupled with advancements in antibiotics, have greatly reduced or eradicated infectious diseases like smallpox or polio, which claimed millions of lives in the past.

Conclusion: Increased Lifespan and Retirement Planning

These advances in healthcare have a profound impact on how we age, retire, and plan for retirement. Our increasing life expectancy, a testament to progress in medical science, requires us to rethink traditional retirement paradigms. Individuals need to plan for longer post-retirement life, manage healthcare costs for chronic illnesses associated with aging, and ensure their finances can accommodate a potential multi-decade retirement.

For many, a longer life also means extending their work years, either by choice or financial necessity. Still, with the appropriate financial planning and understanding of the changing retirement landscape, we can view increased life expectancy not as a challenge but as an opportunity to enjoy a longer, fuller life. The chance to explore passions, spend time with loved ones, and even start new career endeavors.

As we reap the benefits of advances in healthcare, we must remember that living longer needn't translate to surviving longer—instead, it can mean thriving in and enjoying the extended time that science and technology have gifted us.

## Economic Reasons for Delayed Retirement

The traditional arc of life—growing up, pursuing an education, establishing a career, and retiring around the age of 65—has been the long-standing norm. However, a shift in economic conditions coupled with increased life expectancy has seen more individuals delaying their retirement. The economic realities driving this trend are multilayered.

Increased Living Costs

One of the most pressing economic reasons for delayed retirement is the steady rise in the cost of living. From housing to healthcare expenses, everything has seen inflation rates outpacing income growth over the years. It's a common sentiment among later-age workers that the savings they once considered adequate seem insufficient today.

Decline in Savings and Investing

Coupled with the rising cost of living, many people are finding themselves with less savings than they anticipated, thanks to the lingering effects of economic recessions and temporary or long-term unemployment. Plus, a growing apprehension of investment risks—driven by the relative recency of financial crises like 2008—has led to a decrease in personal investments, limiting growth potential for many retirement portfolios.

Vanishing Pensions and the Shift Towards Personal Investment Responsibility

The past few decades have signaled the end of the "golden era" of pensions. Long gone are the days when workers could rely on a hefty pension from a corporation after 30 or so years of service. Many companies have phased out or significantly reduced their pension plans in favor of defined contribution plans like 401(k)s. This shift transfers the duty of retirement saving from employers to employees, increasing the financial burden on individuals planning for retirement.

Lower Interest Rates

In response to various economic crises over the years, the Federal Reserve has held interest rates at historically low levels to stimulate economic growth. While these lower interest rates are beneficial for borrowers, they adversely impact retirees relying on fixed-income investments. With traditional interest-earning accounts yielding little, if any, return, people might be compelled to work longer to compensate for the lost income.

Longer Life Expectancy

People are living longer thanks to advancements in healthcare, which means retirement savings need to last longer. The fear of outliving their savings—longevity risk—drives many to postpone retirement.

Lack of Adequate Healthcare Coverage

Healthcare expenses are a major concern for retirees. Despite Medicare availability, many healthcare costs are out-of-pocket expenses—dental care, hearing aids, long-term care—that can add up quickly. Therefore, continuous employment, which often provides essential health insurance benefits, is increasingly attractive to older adults.

The Reality of Debt

Older generations are carrying significant debt into their retirement years, mostly due to mortgages and increases in education loans for their children. This financial burden necessitates extended work years to reduce these debts.

While these economic realities might seem daunting, they highlight the importance of sound financial planning and adaptability. With the emergence of gig economy opportunities and the possibility of second or third careers, many are finding ways to make the most of these extended work years. With strategic planning and an embrace of lifelong learning, navigating these economic changes is possible. Having the right retirement plan to suit these changes ensures financial resilience to weather the increasing uncertainties of the retirement landscape.

## The Psychological and Social Impact of Extended Working Years

The possibility of extended working years brought about by shifting retirement paradigms can yield both positive and negative effects. Understanding these impacts at the psychological and social level is crucial to manage the retirement transition effectively and ensure a satisfactory quality of life.

### Psychological Impact

On one hand, prolonged employment can provide a psychological boost. Work often gives people a sense of purpose and validation, and it can be beneficial for mental acuity. Staying engaged and challenged by one's work can stimulate the brain, which may delay cognitive decline and reduce the risk of

Alzheimer's disease and dementia in old age.

Moreover, work can provide a structured lifestyle, giving individuals a routine and a reason to be productive each day. This structured lifestyle can lend itself to maintaining better physical health and thus, better psychological well-being.

However, on the downside, extended work years can take a toll on mental health. Job stress doesn't disappear with age—it might even intensify. The pressure to keep pace with younger workers, keep up with technological advances, or handle a heavy workload can all potentially add to stress, leading to anxiety or depression.

In addition, extended working years can infringe on the leisure time that retirees eagerly look forward to. Those who continue working might feel that they're missing out on activities they hoped to enjoy more in their golden years—travel, hobbies, time with family. This perceived loss of leisure can lead to a sense of regret or disappointment.

Social Impact

The social implications of working longer also present a mixed bag. Workplace connections often contribute significantly to an individual's social network. Prolonged employment allows for the maintenance of these relationships, which can be beneficial as relationships are considered protective factors in aging.

Continued working can also foster intergenerational connections, which could lead to unique friendships and mentorships that cut across age boundaries, contributing to a greater sense of social cohesion.

However, depending on the work environment, older workers might face ageism, feel disconnected from younger colleagues, or feel undervalued. This can negatively impact their social integration and self-esteem. Not to mention, retirement typically signifies a time to enjoy life beyond work. Delayed retirement may defer dreams of traveling, spending time with grandchildren, or participating more in community events and could even strain personal relationships.

In conclusion, the psychological and social impacts of delaying retirement are complex and individual. Each person's experience will depend on several factors like their job type and satisfaction, personality, health, financial situation, and social support systems. As retirement spans increasing years of older adulthood, it's crucial to prioritize mental health and social connections and determine what an enjoyable and fulfilling retirement looks like on an individual level. Planning for extended working years isn't just about financial stability, but also about ensuring a balanced lifestyle and quality of life.

# CHAPTER 2: THE NEW ECONOMIC LANDSCAPE

# THE RISE OF THE GIG ECONOMY AND ITS IMPLICATIONS

## *The Gig Economy: Definition*

The gig economy—also referred to as the freelance, platform, share, or temporary job economy—is an increasingly prevalent labor market characterized by short-term contracts or freelance work as opposed to permanent jobs. It revolves around the idea of flexible, project-based, at-will work engagements, where workers become 'gig' performers, each 'gig' being a single job or assignment.

Understood broadly, the gig economy encompasses a wide array of workers ranging from freelance designers to Uber drivers, from seasoned consultants to handyman services. These individuals are not employees of any firm, but rather independent contractors who perform work on a project-by-project basis, often leveraging technological platforms for matching their services with those who need them.

The Origins of the Gig Economy

The origins of the gig economy can be traced back through several parallel trajectories, where cultural, economic, and technological factors coalesced to shape its development.

Economically, the gig economy could arguably be seen as a response to the fallout from the economic recession of 2008. During this period, businesses were looking to cut costs, and one of the ways they found to achieve this was by hiring contractors and freelancers instead of full-time employees, thereby saving on benefits and other associated costs of direct employment. At the same time, many workers were experiencing job loss or reduced job security, leading some to turn to freelance or temporary work as a means of income.

Culturally, societal shifts towards valuing autonomy, flexibility, and individualism have also fueled the gig economy. The concept of a 'job for life' has gradually eroded over the last few decades, and many workers, particularly millennials and subsequent generations, appreciate the freedom, flexibility, and personal fulfillment offered by gig work.

Technologically, the birth and growth of the gig economy have been inextricably linked with the advent and rise of the internet. The digital revolution has facilitated this mode of working by making it possible to work remotely, share resources, connect employers with freelancers quickly, and promote one's skills to a broad audience.

Platforms like Uber, Airbnb, TaskRabbit, Fiverr, and Upwork, to name a few, have capitalized on these technological advancements. They have created a marketplace where services can be traded on an unprecedented scale. From ridesharing and food delivery to graphic design and coding, these platforms have virtually made 'enterprising oneself' possible in myriad ways.

The gig economy, growing out of a confluence of cultural,

technological, and economic shifts, has significantly changed the landscape of work. As this trend shows no sign of slowing down, it becomes increasingly important to understand its implications on economic practices, retirement planning, and indeed on our very perception of work and life.

## Benefits and challenges faced by gig workers

Benefits of the Gig Economy

Freedom and Flexibility: Undoubtedly, the most highlighted benefit of gig work is its considerable scope for flexibility. Gig workers can often choose when, where, and how they work. This freedom can be a significant advantage for those who prefer scheduling their work around other commitments or hobbies. Many gig workers also enjoy the freedom of choice in the assignments they take on, allowing them to do the work that they find most engaging and rewarding.

Diversified Income Streams: Gig economy workers often have the opportunity to cultivate multiple income streams. Instead of depending solely on the paycheck from a single job, they can patch together various gigs into an income quilt. This 'income diversification' can potentially impart financial resilience, particularly during periods of economic uncertainty.

Entrepreneurial Opportunities: The gig economy provides a platform for entrepreneurial individuals to showcase their skills, develop their brand, and grow their own businesses. By offering their services to a variety of clients, they build experience, networks, and reputation—components crucial to any thriving venture.

Building Skills: The necessity of juggling multiple roles and responsibilities allows gig workers to acquire a plethora of skills. From marketing and customer service to negotiation and time management, gig workers are often on an accelerated learning curve.

However, while the benefits are appealing, it's critical to balance this with an understanding of the challenges often faced by those in the gig economy.

Challenges Faced by Gig Workers

Inconsistent Incomes: The freelance nature of gig work impacts financial stability, presenting one of the most significant challenges faced by gig workers. The feast-and-famine cycles often reported by them are a stark contrast from the consistent monthly paychecks of permanent employment.

Lack of Benefits: In most countries, gig workers, classified as independent contractors, miss out on the benefits enjoyed by full-time employees—health insurance, sick leaves, vacation pay, retirement contributions, and overtime pay, to name a few.

Career Progression Uncertainties: Traditional employment often furnishes a clear career pathway, with possibilities of promotions and increments. Such structured career progressions are typically absent in gig work.

Isolation: Gig workers often operate in isolation, missing out on the camaraderie and networking opportunities that traditional workplaces offer. This isolation can sometimes lead to feelings of disconnection and affect mental well-being.

Limited Legal Protection: Present labor laws in many countries do not adequately extend protection to gig workers. As a result, they often cannot avail of legal recourse in instances of exploitation or unfair practices.

Understanding the benefits and challenges of the gig economy becomes crucial in planning for a secure future. While the gig economy offers a plethora of opportunities, gig workers need to be savvy in navigating the uncertainties and risks associated with it—making it an essential aspect to consider when crafting retirement plans in the AI era.

**The Intersection of AI and Freelance Platforms**

The advent of Artificial Intelligence (AI) has dramatically altered the landscape of the gig economy. AI-driven platforms, algorithms, and tools have invariably influenced the freelance workscape, shaping its trajectory and dictating its evolution. This intersection of AI and freelance platforms manifests itself in various ways, hold significant implications for the gig workers, their clients, and the economy at large.

AI and the Gig Work Matching Process

Freelance platforms, driven by AI algorithms, have significantly streamlined the process of matching gig workers with potential clients. Whether it's Upwork's job success score, Fiverr's performance-based rankings, or TaskRabbit's 'smart matching' feature, AI plays a pivotal role in these platforms by analyzing skills, ratings, availability, and even behavioral indicators to direct job postings to the most suitable candidates. This convenience factor appeals to both clients, who can now efficiently find the right person for the job, and freelancers, who can readily identify the assignments that best suit their areas of expertise and interest.

AI's Role in Facilitating Remote Work

AI-powered tools, especially those for project management, productivity enhancement, and real-time communication, have made it easier than ever for gig workers and their clients to collaborate remotely. Platforms like Slack and Asana, powered by AI, offer streamlined communication and task management, supporting smooth project execution. This not only expands the geographical scope for gig workers but also opens up the global talent pool for employers and businesses.

AI in Payment and Contract Terms

Freelance platforms often use AI to ensure transparent and conducive terms of engagement between freelancers and their clients. AI can analyze large datasets to suggest fair pricing rates, automate contracts, and assist with dispute resolution. Payments too, are more secure, with platforms using machine learning algorithms to protect against fraud and cyber threats.

Sharing Economy and AI

AI is also integral to the success of 'sharing economy' platforms like Uber and Airbnb. AI algorithms, dealing with supply and demand metrics, dynamic pricing models, and customer preference insights, facilitate smooth operations in these sectors. While the benefits they offer are many, they also offer snapshots of the challenges gig workers face in an AI-driven environment, including job insecurity and algorithmic control.

AI and Future of Work

As AI continues to progress, its capabilities stretch into areas of creative thought and complex problem-solving, breaching territories once deemed exclusive to humans. This brings to the table concerns about job security and the obsolescence of certain skills. On the flip side, AI also opens the door to new work opportunities revolving around AI technology itself - which includes roles like AI Ethics Officers, Data Scientists, Machine Learning Engineers, and AI Trainers.

While the intersection of AI and freelance platforms presents a host of opportunities, it also brings forth substantial challenges for the gig workers. The growing reliance on and prevalence of AI necessitates a new approach towards work, requiring adaptability, continuous learning, and financial resilience. Without a doubt, these AI-induced changes and uncertainties must be effectively incorporated into planning for a future-proof retirement.

# AI'S INFLUENCE ON THE GLOBAL ECONOMY AND JOB MARKET

## *Industries most affected by AI advancements*

Artificial Intelligence has undoubtedly induced transformative shifts across multiple sectors, becoming a driving force of innovation, optimization, and efficiency. The sectors most impacted by AI are diverse, ranging from healthcare and finance to manufacturing and retail. In this era of rapid technological evolution, an examination of AI's influence in different industries can help provide a holistic outlook on our future, as well as hold crucial implications for retirement planning.

Healthcare

The healthcare sector is at the forefront of AI adoption, and for a compelling reason: AI can significantly augment the capabilities of doctors, health professionals, and healthcare services. AI-driven applications in healthcare include disease diagnosis with machine learning algorithms, robotic surgeries, personalized medicine based on genetic profiles, AI-driven mental health apps, and predictive analytics for disease outbreaks. AI algorithms equipped with deep learning techniques can 'learn' from thousands of patient records, identify patterns, and predict the disease's progression, leading to early intervention and better patient outcomes.

Manufacturing

AI has revolutionized the manufacturing industry by introducing 'smart factories' that optimize efficiency, reduce waste, and enhance productivity. These factories deploy AI-driven robotics, IoT sensors, and automation software to augment human capabilities on the production line. Predictive maintenance, powered by AI, anticipates potential mechanical failures and mitigates downtime.

Finance

The financial industry's embrace of AI can be seen in customizing portfolio management, automating credit scoring processes, predicting market trends, and preventing fraud. AI-driven robo-advisors are guiding individuals towards personalized investment strategies, optimizing retirement savings goals based on an individual's risk tolerance, and time horizon. Many banking institutions use AI to enhance customer service through intelligent virtual assistants or chatbots.

Retail

The retail industry relies on AI for enhancing the customer experience, predicting shopping behavior, and managing logistics. AI is also making strides in streamlining inventory management and driving sales through personalized recommendations and targeted marketing.

## Transportation and Logistics

AI's imprint is visible in transportation through self-driving cars, intelligent traffic management systems, and efficient route planning. In the logistics domain, AI is used for demand predictability, optimization of delivery pathways, and improving warehouse efficiency with autonomous robots.

## Media and Entertainment

Through personalized content suggestions to harnessing Big Data for audience segmentation and targeting, AI is reshaping the media and entertainment industry. AI-driven tools help in rendering visual effects and in the creative process of content generation.

## Education

AI's impact on education is palpable in areas like personalized learning, predictive analytics to track student progress, intuition of learning difficulties, and AI-powered tutoring systems.

There is hardly an industry untouched by AI's game-changing capabilities. While AI's advancements offer numerous opportunities, they also challenge existing job roles and demand upgraded skills. As such, understanding these AI-induced shifts in various industries is a vital component for anyone planning their retirement in the AI era. Such understanding allows people to anticipate skill demands, adapt accordingly, and maintain financial resilience through periods of rapid technological change.

## Potential Economic Growth and Areas of Stagnation Due to AI

Economic growth is fundamental to living standards, societal progress, and financial stability. In today's interconnected world economy, technological advancements - particularly in the field of Artificial Intelligence - play a pivotal role in shaping growth trajectories. The potent combination of machine learning, cognitive computing, natural language processing, and AI algorithms is driving innovation, pushing productivity boundaries, and transforming traditional economic landscapes.

Potential Economic Growth Areas -

1. **Healthcare**: The road to AI-enhanced healthcare represents a vast economic opportunity. With AI's potential to revolutionize personalized medicine, predictive diagnostics, genome sequencing, drug research, and telemedicine, the sector offers copious growth potential. AI-enabled smart health systems could save healthcare costs and improve patient outcomes, translating into significant economic gains.

2. **E-Commerce**: By hyper-personalising the customer experience, AI not only drives sales but also paves the way for new business models in the e-commerce sector. AI's ability to predict consumer behaviour leads to effective targeting and better conversion rates, igniting substantial economic growth in the process.

3. **Manufacturing**: AI-driven manufacturing, also known as Industry 4.0, is anticipated to lead to an upsurge in productivity and efficiency by integrating AI, IoT, robotics, and high-speed data analytics.

4. **Financial Services**: AI's influence on financial services can boost economic growth by refining risk assessments, managing assets more effectively, streamlining regulatory compliance and enhancing customer experience.

5. **CapTech**: Capitalizing on AI to drive technological innovation in the public sector, or GovTech, is another promising area with potential for economic expansion. With AI streamlining bureaucratic processes and driving efficiencies, the public sector's digital transformation could lead to significant cost savings and economic rewards.

Potential Areas of Stagnation -

Despite the many benefits, AI can also catalyze areas of economic stagnation. Timely identification of these sectors can inform both government policy and personal career planning.

1. **Jobs at risk of automation**: Certain industries face potential slowdown due to their higher susceptibility to AI-driven automation. These may include traditional retail, manufacturing jobs involving repetitive tasks, call centres, data entry roles, and transportation, owing to advances in self-driving vehicles.

2. **Data Privacy Concerns**: As businesses become more reliant on AI, threats to data privacy could increase, potentially constraining the development of industries reliant on personal data. Regulatory constraints in response to these issues may hamper growth in sectors such as digital marketing, personalized health care, and algorithmic finance.

3. **Digital Divide**: A lack of equal access to technology

or a lack of digital literacy can also lead to stagnation. Sectors dependent on a wide consumer base's digital participation may experience slower growth if a significant segment of the population is cut off from these advancements.

4. **Need for continuous upskilling**: Not all sectors can adapt to the pace of AI advancements, leading to slower growth. Businesses, particularly small and medium enterprises, may struggle to afford or implement AI, leading to a competitive disadvantage and possible stagnation.

The intersection of AI and economic growth is a dynamic landscape. By focusing not only on the islands of growth but also understanding areas at risk of stagnation, we can create balanced strategies for personal career planning, industry investment, and public policy, enabling us to shape a more inclusive, resilient, and growth-centric AI-enhanced economic landscape.

## Rethinking Job Security and Skills in Demand

The rise of artificial intelligence (AI), historical and ongoing, represents both a remarkable technological achievement and a profound societal challenge. In particular, as AI technology continues its upward trajectory, the narrative around job security is fundamentally shifting.

Latch onto the fact that AI hasn't only created new industries, products, and services on a grand scale, but it also has the potential to automate certain tasks, leading to displacement in job sectors. Thus, the traditional concept of job security is being reconsidered, leading to new strategies for career progression and skills development.

Just a few years ago, job security was synonymous with a steady, full-time job, preferable with a lifelong employment promise. Today, in an AI-driven economy, this notion is quickly becoming outdated. Automation has begun to influence several sectors, performing routine tasks with speed and accuracy beyond human capabilities. Contrarily, AI has also created promising new job categories and industries that we couldn't even fathom just a decade ago.

Such dynamism presents a seismic shift in how we consider job security. Herein, it's no longer about obtaining protected employment for life, but more about building a repertoire of transferable, hard-to-automate skills and a willingness to learn and adapt continually. Simply put, job security is no more a passive state; it now demands active participation and adaptability.

The broad consensus among economists and technologists is that while AI may automate certain tasks, it can't replace the complex problem-solving abilities, critical thinking, creativity, and human-centric skills that we bring to the table. These, along with AI literacy, are becoming increasingly valuable as we navigate the future job market. This shift places a premium on skills that are uniquely human, calling for a radical transformation in how we perceive work, value skills, and plan our careers.

Skills in Demand -

1. **AI and Machine Learning Skills**: As AI continues to invade the job market, there is a growing demand for professionals skilled in AI and machine learning. Please note, it's not only about creating AI but also understanding its application, ethics, and potential.

2. **Data Literacy**: In an AI-dominated economy, data is the new oil. As such, being fluent in data—how to analyze it, draw insights from it and make data-driven decisions—is a critical skill.

3. **Emotional Intelligence (EI)**: Robots may beat us in computation, but they can't replicate our capacity for empathy, understanding, and emotional connection. As AI continues to take over technical tasks, jobs requiring high emotional intelligence are likely to remain in demand.

4. **Critical Thinking and Innovation**: In a rapidly evolving landscape, the ability to solve complex problems, think outside the box, and innovate is ever more critical.

5. **Tech Savviness**: As our world becomes more digitally interconnected, the ability to use new technologies and understanding their impact becomes a fundamental skill.

6. **Adaptability and Flexibility**: In the face of constant change, the ability to learn new skills, unlearn outdated ones, and relearn continually will separate those who thrive from those left behind.

To meet the AI era's challenges, there is a pressing need to rethink our education and training systems. Lifelong learning must become the norm rather than the exception. Governments, educational institutions, and employers must initiate active mechanisms for continuous learning and re-skilling. All the while, individuals should take ownership of their personal growth and adaptability.

Ultimately, in an AI-enhanced world, the linchpin of job security rests on our ability to reframe our notion of it, incessantly learn new skills, and adapt to the changing landscape. As the adage goes, change is the only constant, and perhaps, it is our ability to change and adapt that will secure our place in the future job market.

# UNDERSTANDING THE UNCERTAINTIES:

## *Historical Perspectives on Economic Fluctuations*

Economic fluctuations, also referred to as business cycles, are a fundamental reality of any economy. These cycles, marked by periods of expansion (growth) and contraction (recession), have been a regular and recurring feature ever since the advent of market-driven economies.

In its simplest form, a business cycle involves an economic downturn marked by falling output and employment, followed by a recovery phase, leading to expansion. While these cycles are almost as old as economies themselves, their causes, impacts, and potential remedies have been a subject of fervent study and debate among economists throughout history.

Cast your mind back to the mid-17th century, economic fluctuations were largely driven by changes in agricultural production, influenced by factors such as weather, war, and disease. The transition into the industrial age in the 18th and 19th centuries resulted in a new paradigm of economic fluctuations. As economies began to industrialize, fluctuations became linked increasingly to investment cycles, with periods of over-investment often leading to economic corrections.

The Great Depression in the 1930s marked a significant turning point in the understanding and management of economic fluctuations. The depth and severity of the Depression led countless economists, most notably John Maynard Keynes, to challenge the classical economic theories, arguing that government intervention is key to stabilizing an economy.

Post World War II, against the backdrop of Keynesian economics, governments worldwide actively began to apply fiscal and monetary policies to mitigate economic fluctuations and maintain high employment levels. However, the oil price shocks in the 1970s and early 1980s led to "stagflation" - a situation of stagnant economic growth coupled with high inflation, thus posing severe challenges to Keynesian theories.

The end of the 20th century and the early part of the 21st century have been characterized by a new type of economic fluctuation, driven largely by financial and technological innovations. The dot-com bubble burst in the early 2000s was a result of over-investment in internet-based companies. This was followed by the global financial crisis of 2008, triggered by a collapse in the subprime mortgage sector in the US, casting a long shadow over global economies.

Today, as we traverse an era characterized by technological disruption, environmental concerns, and now a global pandemic, the nature of economic fluctuations continues to evolve. We are witnessing, in real-time, the economic impact and recovery patterns of a singular event – the COVID-19 pandemic. While economists grapple with questions concerning recovery trajectories (Will it be V-shaped? U-shaped? W-shaped?), one fact remains crystal clear - economic fluctuations remain omnipresent, intricately woven into the fabric of our economies.

These historical perspectives underscore two significant points about economic fluctuations. Firstly, economies have continuously evolved, driven by factors such as technological advances, changes in government policies, and global events. Secondly, while it's impossible to fully predict and prevent these fluctuations, they can be managed. Learning from historical patterns, adopting sound economic policies, investing in economic resilience, and ensuring institutional robustness can go a long way in mitigating the impacts of such fluctuations.

As we reflect on the past and prepare for future economic fluctuations, the role of AI in predicting and managing these cycles comes into focus. As we delve deeper into the AI Era, carries the promise of providing us with more nuanced, accurate, and timely tools for economic forecasting and decision-making, thereby equipping us to face economic uncertainties with greater confidence and resilience.

**Projecting the Unpredictable: AI's Role in Financial Forecasting**

In the financial world, the ability to anticipate and respond to market changes is both a boon and a challenge. Traditional methods of financial forecasting have striven to solve this conundrum using human intelligence and ingenuity. However, the advent of artificial intelligence (AI) technologies promises to revolutionize this process, unlocking greater predictive accuracy and providing actionable insights to shape future financial strategies.

Underlying AI's potential in financial forecasting are advancements in machine learning (ML), a subset of AI that enables computers to learn, adapt, and make decisions from data. Through ML algorithms, financial forecasting has transitioned from simply analyzing historical data to identifying patterns, trends, and correlations in real-time. This shift from descriptive analytics (what happened?) to predictive analytics (what could happen?) and prescriptive analytics (how can we make it happen?) is a testament to AI's transformative impact.

AI-powered financial forecasting can help anticipate and manage economic fluctuations in numerous ways:

1. Enhanced accuracy: AI algorithms can sift through vast datasets - including financial markets, macroeconomic indicators, social media sentiment, political events - to generate accurate and up-to-date forecasts. Human analysts, while invaluable, may miss subtle correlations in these datasets that AI can detect.

2. Real-time insights: AI allows for real-time data analysis, ensuring immediate adjustments to forecasts as new data comes in. This ability is paramount in today's fast-moving financial markets.

3. Scenario generation and analysis: AI can quickly generate and evaluate different scenarios based on changes in various parameters. This capability allows financial advisors and investors to stress-test their financial strategies against different potential future outcomes and assess their resilience.

4. Personalization: As AI increasingly evolves, so does its ability to tailor forecasts to individual needs. Such personalization is critical in retirement planning, where individual risk tolerance, financial goals, and life circumstances significantly influence financial strategies.

Despite these advantages, it's crucial to consider potential pitfalls. An AI algorithm is only as good as the data it's trained on; biases in data can lead to inaccurate forecasts and, consequently, poor financial decisions. Moreover, while AI can provide powerful insights, it does not negate the need for human judgement or understanding the broader socio-economic context. Factors such as policy changes, social unrest, or pandemics - fundamentally human and unpredictable elements - still warrant human intuition and experience to complement AI forecasts.

The blending of AI in financial forecasting promises a more robust and sophisticated approach to managing economic fluctuations. Grasping this, we can better navigate unfamiliar terrains, assuage uncertainties about the future, and equip ourselves to craft a resilient and secure retirement. As we venture into this AI-driven era, our ability to effectively marry technological prowess with human ingenuity and instinct will be what truly futureproofs our financial well-being.

24)Building a resilient retirement plan amidst uncertainties:

## 24) Building a Resilient Retirement Plan Amidst Uncertainties

Retirement planning in a rapidly evolving technological landscape, shaped by factors such as AI advancements, market volatility, and inflationary trends, necessitates a robust and versatile strategy - one that anticipates and effectively meets changing conditions. Navigating such complexities can be daunting, but armed with AI-driven financial acumen and traditional financial planning expertise, we can construct resilient retirement plans robust against uncertainty. Here's how:

1. **Diversification:** An age-old adage, 'do not put all your eggs in one basket' is critical in retirement planning. Diversifying your portfolio across asset classes, sectors, and geographies can help manage potential losses and exploit growth opportunities. AI-driven tools can assist in this regard, analyzing market trends to suggest optimal diversification strategies.

2. **Regular Reviews and Realignment:** Retirement plans are not 'set and forget.' With shifting economic conditions, personal circumstances, and life goals, regular review and realignment of your portfolio are necessary. Here again, AI can augment such efforts, offering real-time insights and proactive advice based on changes in personal or market circumstances.

3. **Long-term Perspective:** While it's tempting to react to short-term market changes, a long-term perspective remains crucial in retirement planning. Over-reacting to market shifts can jeopardize the growth of your nest egg. AI forecasting tools can help provide clarity by simulating long-term implications of different market scenarios on your portfolio.

4. **Inflation Hedge:** An unabating reality, inflation slowly erodes purchasing power over time - a significant concern for retirement planning. Investing in assets with the potential to outpace inflation, such as equities or real estate, can offer some protection. While these investment avenues come with their own risks, AI-based tools can help assess these risks and suggest optimal investment pathways.

5. **Adequate Liquidity:** Ensuring an element of liquidity in your retirement portfolio to handle unexpected costs is vital. Immediate medical expenses, home repairs, or family emergencies necessitate access to cash without disrupting your investment plans. Here, AI-based robo-advisors can help

assess your liquidity needs, anticipating short-term cash requirements, and suggesting liquid fund options.

6. **Insurance and Annuity products:** These can offer a safety net by providing stable income streams and covering unforeseen medical or life hazards. With numerous products available on market, AI-powered comparative tools can assist in selecting the best policy tailored to your needs and circumstances.

7. **Embrace Learning and Adaptability:** Lastly, adaptability characterizes a resilient retirement plan. Whether it's learning to use new AI-driven financial tools, or adjusting your financial strategies to global changes, adaptability ensures your retirement plan evolves with your changing lifecycle needs, aiding in sustaining uncertainties.

While uncertainties may appear as formidable challenges, they can be effectively navigated with a blend of AI technology and core financial planning principles. As we embrace this modern era, where humans and machines operate in symbiosis, we have the potential to craft retirement plans that are as resilient as they are secure, enabling us to face the uncertain future with confidence and peace of mind.

# CHAPTER 3: THE AI-ENHANCED RETIREMENT TOOLS

# MODERN TOOLS FOR FINANCIAL PLANNING AND WEALTH MANAGEMENT

## *Overview of popular AI-driven financial tools*

In the modern era marked by unprecedented technological advances, artificial intelligence (AI) has emerged as a game-changer in multiple domains, particularly the financial sector. AI-driven financial tools are not only redefining retirement planning but also revolutionizing it, making complex financial maneuvers easily accessible to everyone. Let's delve into some of the popular AI-driven financial tools that are at the forefront:

1. **Robo-Advisors:** Pioneering the AI revolution in financial planning are the robo-advisors. Armed with AI algorithms, these digital financial advisors help users achieve optimal asset allocation based on specific risk tolerance, financial goals, and projected investment horizon. Major players like Betterment, Wealthfront, and Vanguard Personal Advisor, are offering comprehensive financial advisory services at a fraction of traditional costs.

2. **AI Investment Platforms:** Innovative AI platforms, such as Wealthsimple, Robinhood, and Stash, are empowering investors to leverage machine learning for decision making. These platforms, by analyzing massive data sets, provide data-backed investment recommendations and asset diversification strategies, which cater to both conservative and risk-taking investors.

3. **AI-Driven Savings Tools:** AI isn't just simplifying investing, it's also enhancing saving. Apps like Digit and Clarity Money use AI to analyze users' spending patterns, savings goals and automatically save optimal amounts whilst providing detailed, insightful financial reports. They essentially function as personal finance assistants, guiding users towards more prudent spending decisions and higher savings rates.

4. **AI-Based Insurance Platforms:** Leveraging AI, modern insurance platforms are demystifying complex insurance products. Platforms like PolicyBazaar, Lemonade, and Insurify use AI to tailor policy recommendations, generate personalized premium quotes, and predict potential risks, all based on users' profiles and preferences.

5. **AI-Driven Credit Score Improvement Tools:** AI tools like Credit Karma and WalletHub not only provide free access to credit scores but also analyze users' financial data to provide personalized tips for improving credit ratings. With better credit scores translating into lower borrowing costs in retirement, these AI tools hold significant value.

6. **AI Blockchain Platforms:** AI and Blockchain, two revolutionary technologies, are also intersecting in platforms like SingularityNET. Such platforms leverage AI's data processing prowess and Blockchain's enhanced security to

let users create, monetize, and trade AI services, boosting individuals' capacity to maintain and grow wealth.

7. **Personalized Learning Platforms:** AI-driven platforms like Investopedia Academy and Udemy offer personalized learning paths in finance and investment. Using AI algorithms, these platforms recommend suitable courses based on users' knowledge level, learning style, and performance in previous courses – empowering individuals with knowledge and confidence to manage their finances effectively.

AI is no longer future tech - it's here, revolutionizing financial planning and retirement strategies across the board. These tools, with their enhanced efficiency, cost-effectiveness, and personalization capabilities, are streamlining financial management, making it accessible, understandable, and empowering for the retiree. As technology continues to rapidly evolve, so too will the potential of AI-driven tools in shaping our economic independence and future prosperity.

**Advantages of AI Integration in Financial Planning**

The world is on the cusp of a technological revolution, and the realm of financial planning is no exception. As artificial intelligence (AI) continues to evolve at an unprecedented pace, it is revolutionizing how individuals plan, manage, and safeguard their retirement funds. By integrating AI into financial planning, startling new possibilities have been thrust open. This chapter explores the multitude of advantages that the incorporation of AI offers in the sphere of financial planning:

1. **Personalization and Customization:** AI excels at processing large volumes of data and extracting meaningful insights from them. It can monitor a client's financial behavior, analyze

market trends, consider lifestyle preferences, and compile a wealth of other demographic, socioeconomic data to generate highly customized financial advice, an exceptional advantage for individuals seeking tailored financial planning.

2. **Greater Efficiency:** Traditional financial planning procedures often involve complicated paperwork, countless meetings, and substantial time commitment. On the contrary, AI-driven financial platforms ensure a seamless experience, conducting real-time financial analysis, and creating instant financial models, thereby dramatically increasing efficiency.

3. **Reduced Costs:** Leveraging AI can significantly reduce costs associated with financial planning. Traditional financial advisors usually charge a percentage of the assets they manage, while AI-driven financial tools come at a fraction of that cost, making professionally designed financial planning accessible to a broader audience.

4. **24/7 Availability:** Unlike human advisors, AI-driven platforms are available round the clock, offering clients the convenience to access financial advice whenever they need. Therefore, even in different time zones or during non-working hours, the financial planning process is never at a standstill.

5. **Improved Risk Assessment:** AI systems are capable of assessing multitudes of risk factors instantly by analyzing vast amounts of data from various sources. They can detect patterns and anomalies that might be difficult for humans to identify, hence enabling a more accurate assessment of investment risks.

6. **Better Predictive Abilities:** Through machine learning and complex algorithms, AI tools can examine past market trends and make highly accurate predictions about future

market behavior. These insights can guide investment decisions, retirement planning, and risk management strategies in a dynamic economic landscape.

7. **Proactive Adjustments:** AI's superior data processing and predictive capabilities enable proactive adjustments to financial plans based on changing market conditions, personal financial situations, or adapted retirement needs. Such flexibility is critical in ensuring a retirement plan stays robust and relevant.

8. **Enhanced Security:** Integrative AI systems can provide added layers of protection against fraudulent activities and cyber threats. They can continuously monitor transactions, identify suspicious activities, and flag potential security risks promptly.

In conclusion, integrating AI into financial planning offers profound benefits that go beyond enhancing efficiency and reducing time and costs. Personalization, proactive adjustments, and enhanced security features are some advantages that AI brings, helping individuals construct a robust and flexible retirement plan. By embracing this technological shift, we stand to create richer, more secure retirements for individuals, and a more inclusive and equitable financial planning landscape for all.

## Potential Pitfalls and What to Watch Out For

Whether it's the integration of a new technology, a paradigm shift, or a seismic economic change, each comes with its unique set of challenges and potential pitfalls. The integration of Artificial Intelligence in financial planning certainly carries numerous advantages, providing facile personalization, improved efficiency, and cost-effectiveness. However, it's equally important to tread cautiously recognizing certain hazards this advancement might harbor. Here are some potential pitfalls and cautionary measures:

1. **Over-reliance on Technology:** One of the significant concerns is the danger of over-reliance on AI. While AI can indeed churn out insightful analyses and facilitate automated decision-making, it's imperative to view this as a tool assisting human judgment, not replacing it. There's no substitute for human critical thinking, especially when handling complex financial matters.

2. **Algorithmic Bias:** The outputs generated by AI are dependent on the data the algorithms have been trained on. If this data is biased, it results in skewed, prejudiced, or unfair decisions, a phenomenon known as 'Algorithmic Bias.' It's crucial to ensure that the AI tools employed are trained on diverse, representative, and unprejudiced data sets.

3. **Data Privacy:** AI-driven financial planning tools require significant personal financial data to operate efficiently. This poses a serious concern about data security and privacy. Ensuring stringent cybersecurity measures and understanding the data handling practices of the AI service provider are essential.

4. **Inadequate Regulation:** Given that AI in financial planning is still a relatively nascent development, regulations and oversight might not be comprehensive, thereby leaving room for malpractices. Before adopting such technologies, checking the regulatory and compliance strength becomes vital.

5. **Lack of Personal Touch:** Financial planning is not solely about numbers; it's also about understanding a client's unique

aspirations, fears, and life circumstances. While AI can certainly personalize at scale, it may still lack the depth of understanding and empathy a human advisor can bring.

6. **Volatile AI Predictions:** Though AI has improved predictive abilities, the market's unpredictable nature may sometimes render these predictions inaccurate. It's crucial to have a risk management strategy in place and not entirely depend on these projections.

7. **Technical Failures:** Like any technological system, AI-driven tools are susceptible to technical failures and glitches, which can lead to major setbacks. Ensuring back-ups and recovery measures, therefore, becomes critical.

Moving forward, while AI undeniably propels us tin the direction of a more streamlined and efficient financial future, it's incumbent upon us to balance this relentless drive for advancement with due caution. As we embrace AI's capabilities, we must also prudently navigate potential pitfalls – an approach that will ensure a more secure, fair, and prosperous retirement future for everyone.

# HOW AI IS PERSONALIZING RETIREMENT PLANS

## *The Role of Data Analytics in Customized Financial Advice*

We live in a divergent and variated world, each individual's financial goals, needs, and perspectives can considerably differ, rending the one-size-fits-all advice far less than optimal. When planning for retirement, it's not only about how much money you'd need, but also when you might require it, what your risk tolerance is, and what your other financial obligations are. The advent of big data analytics and its integration with Artificial Intelligence is changing this narrative and ushering in an era of highly personalized financial advice tailored to an individual's unique set of requirements.

1. **Assessment of Financial Status and Goals**: Firstly, data analytics assists in gathering comprehensive data about an individual's financial status. This includes income, expenses, savings, debts, investments, etc. Personal goals, such as buying a house, funding children's education, travel plans, and importantly, the individual's retirement dreams, are recorded. This data serves as the raw material based on which customized financial advice is formulated.

2. **Risk Profiling**: Based on data from various sources, data analytics can help create a unique risk profile for each individual. This profile takes into account not just financial risk capacity (based on income, wealth, and dependency) but also the individual's risk tolerance (psychological willingness to take risk assessed through specially designed questionnaires or AI-driven psychometric tests). Algorithms then match this risk profile with suitable investment options.

3. **Predictive Analytics and Personalization**: Machine Learning, a subset of AI, thrives on data. The more they get, the more they 'learn' and improve. Based on the historical data of an individual's expenses, income pattern, investments, and various financial behaviors, predictive models can forecast future financial requirements and accordingly suggest the optimal saving and investment strategies. This prediction is not static; instead, it continually adjusts as new data flows in, thereby helping modify financial plans in tune with changing circumstances.

4. **Scenario Analysis and Stress Testing**: Big Data can help simulate various financial scenarios and carry out stress testing to check the robustness of the financial plan in adverse situations. This helps clients understand the potential risks associated with their financial decisions and ensures that they are better prepared for unexpected market turns or life events.

5. **Automated Personal Financial Advisory**: Robo-advisors powered by AI and data analytics make personalized financial advice accessible and affordable for everyone. They use algorithms to dish out financial advice and automate investing based on individual needs and risk profiles, thereby bringing in a democratization of sorts in the personal financial advisory domain.

Although data analytics continues to revolutionize the landscape of personalized financial advice, it bears reminding that like any technology, it's purely a tool. It needs to be calibrated in line with the ethical considerations and regulatory norms and should have the necessary checks and balances in place to ensure security and privacy. Most importantly, despite the high degree of personalization it offers, it should complement, not substitute, the human connection, judgement, understanding, and empathy – elements unwaveringly critical in the sensitive world of personal finance. AI and data analytics must serve as enablers on the path to a fulfilling and secure retirement, empowering individuals to realize their financial dreams in the golden years of their lives.

**Case Studies: AI-Driven Success Stories in Retirement Planning**

In recent years, we have seen a plethora of applications of Artificial Intelligence (AI) in the domain of retirement planning. AI's transformative potential is helping shape more secure retirements, respond to unexpected market upheavals, and offer tailor-made retirement solutions. Let's delve into a few real-world case studies that reflect the triumphant alliance of AI and retirement planning.

1. **Betterment, Robo-Advisor Success Story**:

Betterment, a robo-adviser platform based in the U.S, uses AI and machine learning to provide personalized investment recommendations. John, a 45-year-old school teacher, began using Betterment to plan for his retirement. The platform evaluated John's risk tolerance by asking him a series of questions. It then recommended a suitable investment portfolio, which comprised of low-cost index funds and bonds, matching his risk profile and retirement timeline. As John factored in new financial goals like his daughter's college fund, Betterment's algorithms adjusted his investment strategies accordingly, ensuring he didn't stray off his primary goal – retirement. An annual return of about 10% testified the success of this AI-driven approach in John's case.

2. **'Pefin' - A Personalized AI Financial Advisor**:

Pefin, an AI-driven platform, offers tailored financial planning services, which include retirement planning. Pefin sketches a full financial life plan that evolves as user situations change. Julia, a 38-year old professional, used Pefin to start strategizing for her retirement. Pefin first computed an in-depth understanding of Julia's current finances, her lifestyle, and future goals. It then used AI algorithms to project her financial future considering inflation, cost of living changes, and market conditions. It helped Julia understand how saving more or retiring at a different age would impact her retirement lifestyle. As Julia progressed in her career and her financial situation changed, Pefin adjusted her retirement plan in real-time. With Pefin's assistance, Julia could make informed decisions about her life and retirement plans confidently.

3. **Vanguard's Personal Advisor Services (PAS)**:

Victoria was a 60-year-old retiree who had her retirement savings spread across various accounts in different banks and financial institutions. Keeping track of assets became an arduous task, and devising a withdrawal strategy was even more tedious. Vanguard's Personal Advisor Services helped Victoria create a simplified and tax-efficient withdrawal strategy with AI algorithms tracking all her retirement accounts. It projected the longevity of her retirement savings considering her lifestyle choices and market conditions, thus offering her peace of mind and financial stability throughout her retired life.

These stories testify to the power of AI in crafting effective, robust, and personalized retirement plans in sync with individual requirements, risk profiles, and life transitions. However, it's important to note that while AI enhances precision and convenience, a baseline human touch is indispensable in managing personal finances and retirement planning. AI should function as a tool to augment and assist human judgment and expertise when it comes to navigating the complex world of retirement planning.

**Future Trends in AI Personalization**

Artificial Intelligence (AI) is reshaping paradigms across several industries, with retirement planning being one of the domains experiencing radical transformations. This is largely due to personalization, the cornerstone of AI accomplishments. Personalized retirement planning, empowered by AI, is about amplifying individuality, acknowledging unique personal profiles, and responding to particular goals or expectations. This trend of personalization in retirement planning is only expected to grow in the future, especially in the following ways:

1. **Hyper-Personalized Financial Counselling**:

Future AI platforms would echo the counsel of a human advisor, aligning advice to the individual's unique circumstances and objectives. These platforms will comprehend the user's financial status, goals, risk tolerance, and lifestyle choices. But beyond that, they will incorporate intangible factors, such as a user's emotional response to volatility, apprehensions about market downturns, and their subjective financial well-being. In essence, retirement planning tools will operate in a way that resembles human conversation far more than an automated response.

2. **Real-time Plan Adjustment**:

Retirement plans must evolve in step with life progression. Consequently, AI tools will increasingly reflect more precise real-time adjustments. For example, an unexpected career move, a sudden illness, a child's marriage, or a downturn in the market could all require immediate recalibration of the retirement plan. The dynamic adjustment and the real-time evolution of retirement plans based on such changes will be a key focus of AI personalization.

3. **AI-Driven Social Security Optimization**:

Future AI models will offer personalized recommendations on the optimal time to claim social security, given an individual's total retirement savings, expected retirement age, lifestyle, and life expectancy. With a plethora of variables shaping this decision, AI's ability to process diverse data-sets swiftly and accurately can guide individuals through this critical facet, minimizing financial uncertainty.

4. **Enhanced and Personalized User Experience**:

Advancements in AI will drive interactions that are more human-friendly, making these technologies a homelier, integral part of retirement planning. For instance, AI chatbots, with their increasing linguistic sophistication and interactivity, may hold personalized and engaging conversations with users regarding their retirement concerns, rendering the process less daunting and more approachable.

5. **Personalized Learning Approach**:

People differ not only in their financial situations but also in their financial literacy levels. Future AI-driven platforms will assess an individual's financial knowledge and cultivate a personalized learning path. This bespoke educational service may include webinars, articles, videos, or quizzes, transforming retirement planning from a challenging task into an empowering learning journey.

6. **Integration with Healthcare Planning**:

As AI continues to make strides in healthcare services, there is a promising scope for the integration of AI-driven healthcare and retirement planning. For instance, AI can personalize healthcare costs predictions based on an individual's health history, lifestyle, and age. This integration would yield a more holistic, accurate, and individualized retirement blueprint.

The future of AI personalization in retirement planning thus appears promising and transformative. Yet, it's essential that we approach this seismic shift with an awareness of the potential challenges, ethical considerations, and the importance of preserving the human element amidst the march of the machines.

# CASE STUDIES: SUCCESS STORIES OF AI-DRIVEN RETIREMENT SOLUTIONS

## *How Retirees Benefitted from AI Recommendations*

As technology continues to transcend boundaries, AI has stepped into the realm of retirement planning, offering insights that humans might overlook or be incapable of processing promptly. It is not an understatement to say that AI is catalyzing an unprecedented revolution in retirement planning, bestowing retirees with outcomes that they once might have only dreamed of. Let us delve into a few instances where retirees have reaped substantial benefits from AI recommendations:

**Case 1**:

Jim, 71, was an individual with conservative risk tolerance, but his retirement investment portfolio didn't align with his preferences. A smart AI-based financial tool detected the incongruity by analyzing his interests, fears, lifestyle, and financial history. It suggested a portfolio rebalancing towards more stable assets like bonds and fixed income securities. Implementing this AI recommendation has helped Jim to spend his retirement without the dread of market fluctuations consuming his peace. His example shows how AI tools can personalize portfolio optimization to a retiree's risk tolerance, helping to better fortify their golden years.

**Case 2**:

Linda, aged 65, was grappling with the big question: when should she start claiming her social security benefits? With various health issues, she was considering taking an early retirement. Using AI predictions on life expectancy based on her health history and long-term prognosis, AI advised her to start claiming benefits earlier. This crucial decision, facilitated by AI tools, allowed her to have a reliable income stream throughout her retirement, ensuring her wellbeing during her twilight years.

**Case 3**:

Take the case of Sam and Jane, both aged 67 and recent retirees, they were keen on globetrotting during their retirement. An interactive personal finance platform driven by AI algorithms, took their unique retirement goals into account. Using real-time data and predictive analytics, the AI designed a unique financial strategy that included travel budgets, inflation factors, and emergency funds. By following these AI recommendations, this couple was able to fulfill their dream of exploring the world without hindering their financial security.

**Case 4**:

Sara, a 69-year-old retiree, was new to the world of finance. Overwhelmed by jargon and complex concepts, she was anxious about her financial future. An AI-driven tool assessed her financial literacy level and identified the knowledge gaps. What followed was a personalized educational journey with bite-sized lessons, tailored to her pace and understanding. As a result, Sara began making informed decisions about her finances independently, thereby ensuring her financial health all through retirement. This case epitomizes the didactic promise of AI, which can make retirement planning an enlightening path rather than a burden.

These success stories attest the potential of AI to transform retirement planning into a more profitable, secure, and stress-free exercise. As retirees continue to benefit from AI's versatile advantages, the technology's role looks set to cement further, shaping the landscape of future retirement planning with its predictive capabilities, seamless customizability, and dynamic adaptability. However, while acknowledging the merits, it remains crucial to be mindful of the novel challenges and ethical implications AI might usher in.

**Lessons Learned and Potential Pitfalls to Avoid**

While AI offers an exciting new frontier for retirement planning, it is not devoid of potential pitfalls. We've examined various case studies where retirees benefitted from AI recommendations, and in each scenario, a specific subset of potential issues was observed. Here are the lessons learned and potential pitfalls to avoid when incorporating AI into retirement planning.

**Communication Gap**:

The case of Jim emphasized the importance of aligning investment portfolios to risk tolerance. However, what if Jim misunderstood the AI recommendations due to complex machine language? An important lesson here is that AI tools must employ clear, human-like language to ensure accurate comprehension of advice and recommendations. Any misunderstanding might lead to poorly informed decisions, compromising the retiree's financial peace.

**Assuming AI's Accurate Life Expectancy Predictions**:

In Linda's case, AI-assisted decisions worked flawlessly. Yet, there lies a potential pitfall: the AI's life expectancy prediction may not always be precise. Medical advancements can prolong life, resulting in costly extended years not factored into the original calculations. Therefore, one mustn't overly rely on AI for such critical decisions without human judgment.

**Reliance on Real-Time Data**:

Sam and Jane's case showed how AI can incorporate retirees' life goals. However, AI's reliability on real-time data could result in hasty financial decisions if the data algorithm was skewed by temporary market or economic volatility. Hence, national and global trends must be given equal consideration while basing retirement plans on AI recommendations.

**Potential for Overconfidence**:

Sara's story was about empowering individuals for informed decisions. However, there's a risk of becoming overconfident in one's ability to handle finances through knowledge provided by AI platforms. Continued professional consultation is still essential, as every financial decision can have multiple tax, risk, and future implications which AI may not be programmed to fully understand or explain.

**Privacy Concerns**:

In all these cases, AI required in-depth personal information for tailored solutions. It raises issues concerning data privacy and security. One must understand how the AI system stores, uses, and shares the sensitive information provided before signing up for such platforms. Anonymized data and robust cyber-security measures are essential to safeguard user privacy.

**AI Bias and Limitations**:

AI isn't free of inherit biases, as the algorithms are ultimately designed by humans. There is a risk of these biases affecting retirees' financial decisions, resulting in less than optimal outcomes. Also, AI, while rapidly advancing, still has its limitations and cannot replace human intuition and experience. Therefore, users need to question AI recommendations critically and supplement them with human advice.

The AI-era has revolutionized retirement planning for the better, opening up many opportunities. Yet, it is also fraught with potential pitfalls that retirees need to be aware of. By understanding these, one can leverage the power of AI cautiously and most effectively in their retirement planning.

## Predictions for the Future of AI-Assisted Retirements

The future of retirement, especially with the integration of Artificial Intelligence, offers an exciting realm of possibilities. As AI continues to evolve, there are certain trends and predictions we can already anticipate.

**Ubiquitous Integration of AI Retirement Tools**:

As AI becomes more sophisticated and accessible, the use of AI-assisted tools in retirement planning is going to be the norm rather than the exception. Traditional financial advisors will either adapt and integrate these tools into their service or risk becoming obsolete. This doesn't signal the end of human advisors but emphasizes a shift towards a strategic advisory role where personal interactions are focused more on a retiree's life goals and holistic financial planning.

**Quicker Real-time Adjustment**:

AI's capability to react and adjust to real-time data will significantly influence future retirement planning. During an economic upheaval or rapid market changes, AI tools can swiftly recalibrate your investment recommendations and retirement strategies. This quick adjustment minimizes the potential losses while opening the doors for potentially profitable opportunities.

**Hyper-Personalization of Retirement Strategies**:

The future of retirement planning will be dictated by the principle of one-size-does-not-fit-all. With AI's ability to analyze massive amounts of data, we can expect an unprecedented level of personalization in retirement strategies. AI will tap into not just financial data, but also lifestyle, career, and health data to draw a comprehensive picture of the retiree's future and craft a commensurate strategy.

**Advances in Predictive Analysis**:

With the advent of more sophisticated AI algorithms, there are likely to be remarkable improvements in predictive analysis. This advancement would significantly impact how we plan for retirement, offering much better precision in predicting investment outcomes, healthcare costs, life expectancy, and more.

**Increased Use of Robo-Advisors**:

Robo-advisors, which are AI-driven wealth management services, have already seen a surge in popularity. Their easy accessibility, lower costs, and intuitive design make them an attractive alternative for retirees. As these platforms become smarter and more efficient, it's plausible they will become a dominant force in retirement management.

**Improved Data Security Measures**:

As reliance on digital technology increases, so does the issue of data privacy and security. There will likely be significant improvements in cybersecurity practices and regulations, ensuring retiree's financial and personal data are safeguarded effectively.

**Regulations and Standards for AI in Retirement Planning**:

As AI becomes integral in retirement planning, we can expect more scrutiny and regulations in the future. These standards and guidelines would be aimed at promoting transparency, combating algorithmic biases, and ensuring ethical practices.

The future of AI-assisted retirements is bright, opening doors for precision, personalization, and ease. Nevertheless, retirees must continue to stay vigilant, adaptable, and informed. They must remain the commander of their retirement ship, using AI as a sophisticated navigator to chart their course to a fulfilling retirement journey.

# CHAPTER 4: PREPARING FOR THE UNEXPECTED

# THE IMPORTANCE OF ADAPTABILITY IN A RAPIDLY CHANGING WORLD

**The Role of Continuous Learning in Modern Retirement**

In the lively dynamics of our technologically-advanced era, the concept of retirement is requiring a significant revamp. As we transition into AI-guided environments, the principle of 'continuous learning' emerges, not just as an optional strategy but a necessity for a fulfilling, modern retirement.

Continuous learning, popularly termed 'lifelong learning,' refers to the pursuit of knowledge for personal and professional development throughout a person's life. It bears immense relevance due to the increasing longevity, frequent career changes, and relentless technological progress in today's life. When it comes to retirement, continuous learning adorns multiple roles; it is a tool for staying relevant, a platform for building social connections, a strategy for financial security, and a path to personal fulfillment.

**Staying Relevant in an AI-Era**:

It is clear that we usher in the age of AI, and staying current with these technologies becomes indispensable, extending well into our golden years. Understanding the latest technologies not only helps retirees better manage their assets through AI-based financial tools but also maintains cognitive health by exercising the 'mental muscles'. Moreover, it provides a sense of relevancy and self-confidence, crucial for psychological wellbeing.

**Building Social Connections**:

Continuous learning platforms, whether online or physical, provide great opportunities to interact with people from different backgrounds and age-groups. For retirees, these interactions may fill the gap left by their departing work-life social structure. Here, they can conceive new friendships, engage in stimulating discussions, and share their experiences, thus enhancing emotional health and avoiding isolation post-retirement.

**Financial Security and Career Opportunities**:

Continuous learning potentially opens the doors for second careers or part-time consulting roles. Harnessing in-demand skills, retirees might launch profitable ventures or embark on fulfilling hobbies that also generate income. In a future steered by AI, jobs requiring uniquely human skills, such as emotional intelligence, creativity, and complex problem-solving, will hold a premium. Continuous learning becomes a conduit to acquire and enhance these skills, offering financial security and purposeful engagement during retirement.

**Personal Fulfillment**:

Finally, and perhaps most importantly, continuous learning serves as a feeder to curiosity, creativity and self-growth. Distanced from the pressures of a full-time job, retirees may utilize this time to learn a musical instrument, delve into art history, crack quantum physics, or master a new language – the options are limitless. This pursuit of passions and interests offers unparalleled personal satisfaction and contributes to a happier, healthier retirement.

In conclusion, our modern era, brightened by AI advancements, beckons a shift in retirement attitudes – from seeing it as the 'end-of-the-line' to embracing it as a rich period of growth and exploration. Continuous learning encapsulates this very spirit and, therefore, should sit at the heart of a modern retirement plan. By embedding learning into lifestyle, retirees can navigate the AI era with strength, stability and satisfaction, rendering an empowering narrative for retirement in the 21st century.

## Strategies for Staying Relevant in an AI-Driven Job Market

In an age where artificial intelligence and technology dominate multiple facets of life, grappling with change and future-proofing employability become central to any retirement strategy. The importance of inclusivity in technological advancements elicits specific strategies for staying relevant, especially for potential retirees in the AI-driven job market. Maintain relevance, financial stability, and safeguard a satisfying retirement by employing these key strategies:

**Embrace Lifelong Learning**

Continuous learning and skill acquisition can't be overstated in the evolving job market. While certain tasks are handed over to AI, the demand for uniquely human skills is noticeably spiking. Emotional intelligence, critical thinking, complex decision-making, creative problem-solving, and people management are some of the skills highly sought after in the AI era. Consider taking online courses, attending workshops, or pursuing additional certification in specific areas to enhance your arsenal of soft skills and technical skills. Studies reveal that adults engaging in lifelong learning exhibit improved cognitive functionality, emotional well-being and, not surprisingly, an increased sense of self-efficacy.

**Leverage Networking and Collaboration**

With the digital sprawl, opportunities to network have grown exponentially. Capitalizing on professional networking platforms, retirees can nurture relationships, foster collaboration, and remain informed about industry trends and job opportunities. Volunteering or participating in community activities can provide opportunities to showcase leadership skills, network, and transition more smoothly into retirement.

**Stay Digitally Updated**

Developing digital literacy is now a must for anyone looking to stay professionally relevant. Simple tasks done manually are now efficiently executed by AI, and staying afloat means getting comfortable with these technological advancements. Whether it's using AI-driven financial tools, adopting project management software, or unlocking efficiencies through automation, a basic understanding of emerging technologies will help maintain your competitive edge in the workforce or as a retiree.

**Adopt a Growth Mindset**

A cornerstone of continuous relevance is the adoption of a 'growth mindset.' It involves embracing challenges, persisting in the face of setbacks, viewing effort as the path to mastery, and learning from criticism. A growth mindset fuels resilience in the face of change, an essential trait in the era of AI and robotics. By fostering a growth mindset, you surefootedly navigate the unpredictable AI sea, remaining adaptable and open to new opportunities.

**Reinvent and Diversify**

Retirement today doesn't signify an abrupt halt of professional activities but rather a transition into new chapters of productivity. One might consider launching a consultancy in their field of expertise, leveraging years of experience to advise businesses or individuals. Others might unlock a dormant entrepreneurial spirit, set up new businesses, or even monetize hobbies.

In essence, remaining relevant in an AI-saturated job market requires a blend of technical acumen, soft skills, and a disposition towards continuous learning. By employing these strategies, potential retirees can confidently craft a rewarding narrative for their retirement, adequately equipped, engaged, and energized in their post-professional life. Seizing the AI era's opportunities, they can steer towards a retirement that is not merely survived but richly lived and enjoyed.

## Building a Flexible Retirement Plan

Even as the wave of technology surges through our lives, one thing remains unchanged – the need for a sound retirement plan. However, the paradigm shift triggered by the AI revolution necessitates a rethink of regular retirement planning, ushering in a new era of flexible retirement plans. Here are several strategies to build such a plan:

**Embrace Diversification**

One of the key tenets of risk management and robust financial planning is diversification. And this rule rings especially true in the context of retirement planning in the AI era. Diversification isn't merely about varying your investment portfolio across equities, bonds, and other asset classes. It also includes investing in various sectors, notably those less vulnerable to AI disruption or even those standing to gain from the AI revolution. This strategy serves to insulate your retirement savings from the unpredictable twists and turns of the market.

**Leverage AI-Based Tools and Platforms**

Financial technology, armed with intuitive AI-based tools, has transformed the face of retirement planning. These intelligent platforms offer personalized retirement plans based on data-driven insights tailored to individual financial goals, risk tolerance, and life expectancy. They can track spending habits, automatically adjust savings rates, and provide real-time feedback, ensuring your retirement plan continues to serve your interest most optimally.

**Retirement Income Planning**

Retirement income planning focuses on generating a regular and reliable cash flow during your retirement years. It involves strategically drawing down from various income sources in a tax-efficient manner, such as social security, annuities, and retirement accounts. Optimizing withdrawals can extend the longevity of your savings and keep up with the increased life expectancy.

**Healthcare and Long-Term Care Provision**

Longer life expectancies, together with the rising costs of healthcare and potential long-term care, pose significant risks to retirees. Including a provision for healthcare costs in your retirement plan helps prevent any potential financial crises that might otherwise eat into your savings.

**Continuous Adjustments and Reviews**

Building a flexible retirement plan is not merely a one-time task. The unpredictable nature of technology, volatile market conditions, ever-changing tax laws, and fluctuating personal circumstances, make it necessary to periodically review and adjust your retirement strategy as needed.

**Embrace Lifelong Learning and Career Flexibility**

Building and maintaining relevant skill sets even in your pre-retirement years could provide supplemental income during retirement and keep you engaged. Additionally, it enables you to adapt to changes in the job market influenced by AI advances, thereby fortifying your future financial security.

**Sequence of Returns Risk Management**

The sequence of investment returns early into retirement can significantly impact your savings' longevity. A downturn in the market during early retirement years can considerably shrink your retirement savings, especially when necessary withdrawals are made. Constructing a retirement plan that mitigates this risk is essential.

A flexible retirement plan in the AI era is not a luxury, but a necessity. By appreciating the implications of AI advancements and forming a fluid strategy that accommodates them, retirees can safeguard their golden years, living them out with financial confidence and personal fulfillment. A carefully structured plan reassures the certainty of a secure and enjoyable retirement, reinforcing the bright side of this beautiful life phase.

# STRATEGIES FOR SAFEGUARDING AGAINST UNEXPECTED COSTS

## *Diversifying Investments and Assets*

As we venture further into the AI Era, the traditional wisdom of diversification - the proverbial advice not to put all your eggs in one basket - takes on an even greater significance. In an environment fraught with uncertainties, keeping a diversified portfolio acts as a safety net, cushioning your retirement plans from the volatility birthed by rapid technological advancements.

**Understanding Diversification**

At its core, diversification is about spreading out investments across various asset categories such as stocks, bonds, real estate, commodities, and cash to reduce risk. The main goal is to maximize return by investing in different sectors that would each react differently to the same event. No single investment or asset class has a tendency to perform well under all economic conditions. Thus, owning a mix of assets will, on balance, increase chances for financial success.

**The Need for Asset Diversification in the AI Era**

AI technology, with its share of profound breakthroughs and disruptions, introduces a new layer of risk and unpredictability to the financial markets. Industries once considered robust might become vulnerable. Top performing companies could be dethroned overnight by tech-driven startups. Given this scenario, betting on a single industry or asset class could jeopardize long-term financial security.

**Harnessing the AI Wave: Diversify across Sectors and Industries**

The AI revolution provides a dual opportunity for diversification – firstly, to protect your investment portfolio from AI-induced disruptions, and secondly, to capitalize on the colossal growth AI technology promises. Diversifying your investments across not just traditional industries, but also ones actively engaging in AI, can help mitigate the downside risk while potentially boosting your retirement corpus.

""Geographical Diversification""

With AI-driven changes affecting economies worldwide, investing solely within your home country presents another set of risks. International diversification, thus, becomes an essential part of a diversified investment strategy.

**Diversification across Time: Dollar-Cost Averaging**

Diversification is not just about diversifying across assets; it's also about diversifying across time. Dollar-cost averaging, which involves consistently investing a fixed sum over time, irrespective of share prices, ensures you buy more shares when prices are low and fewer when high, thus mitigating risk.

**Beware of Over-Diversification**

Just as having all of one's savings in a single asset class poses a risk, it's crucial to avoid over-diversification, which can dilute potential gains. It's essential to strike a delicate balance by selecting a diverse array with a rational number of investments.

In conclusion, diversification is an absolutely indispensable part of any savvy investor's toolkit. It not only spreads risk but also facilitates capitalizing on the volatile nature of markets in the AI era. A well-diversified portfolio can result in a more robust and resilient retirement plan, better equipped to weather the twists and turns of a fast-changing digital world. While no single strategy guarantees success, diversifying your assets goes a long way in aligning your retirement plan with your long-term objectives and risk tolerance, ensuring a secure retirement in this brave new world.

## The Role of Insurance in the Age of AI

As we immerse ourselves deeper into the era defined by the rapid growth of artificial intelligence, traditional sectors of our economy, including insurance, are undergoing a sea change. Varied facets of the insurance business, from underwriting and pricing to fraud detection and claim processing, are being enhanced and, in some cases, entirely reshaped by AI. In this context, understanding how this transformation impacts your retirement planning becomes essential.

**AI and the Insurance Industry: A Perfect Pair**

The insurance industry is inherently data-driven. A plethora of data is analyzed to determine risk and price policies. AI's ability to crunch massive datasets in a fraction of the time taken by traditional analytical methods is a game-changer, enabling insurance companies to build better risk models, personalize policies, and reduce operational costs. These advantages not only translate to cheaper and more efficient service for consumers but also pave the way for innovative insurance products tailored for the digital age.

**The AI-Driven Revolution in Insurance Products**

AI is not just streamlining operations for insurance companies; it's also catalyzing creative solutions that have a direct impact on the consumer. From usage-based car insurance that adjusts premiums based on driving behavior tracked by IoT devices to health insurance products that reward healthy lifestyle choices, AI is personalizing insurance like never before.

**Insurance Planning in the Age of AI**

Given the ever-evolving nature of risks in our digital world, retirement planning today involves more than just safeguarding your nest egg from market volatility. It also entails protection from a host of other modern perils like cyber-attacks, identity theft, and even the unjustified impact of algorithmic decision-making. Here, AI is a double-edged sword. While it presents risks and uncertainties, it also offers solutions to help manage these very risks.

**AI's Role in Building an Effective Insurance Portfolio**

A well-structured insurance portfolio is a fundamental element of a robust retirement plan. AI's predictive analytics tools can help you build this by providing tailored insights about the types of coverage you might need, based on lifestyle variables, personal preferences, life stage, and risk tolerance. By leveraging AI, you can ensure that you're not underinsured or over-insured, but just right.

**AI and Long-Term Care Insurance**

Perhaps one of the areas where AI brings the most dramatic shift in retirement planning is the sphere of Long-Term Care (LTC) insurance. With advanced data analytics and predictive modeling, AI can streamline underwriting for LTC, making the process faster, less intrusive, and potentially less costly for retirees.

**Agents of the Future: AI Chatbots**

The rise of AI has given rise to AI-powered chatbots, which can dispense advice promptly and accurately, and handle claims and policy renewals efficiently, freeing consumers from the chore of navigating overwhelming insurance jargon. While human agents are far from obsolete, the AI-assisted customer service experience can simplify insurance management for retirees.

In this era, where AI is revolutionizing the insurance industry, the role of insurance in retirement planning is not only about protection but also about leveraging this technology to get the best coverage your hard-earned savings can buy. AI presents a horizon of possibilities for consumers, and with careful assessment and consideration, insurance can be a crucial instrument in your arsenal, hedge against various risks in the AI era, and to secure a fulfilling and worry-free retirement.

## Setting Aside Emergency Funds: How Much and Where?

Establishing an emergency fund is foundational to a sound retirement strategy, and its importance can't be overstated in the era where AI dominates financial planning. While market shifts and economic downturns are inevitable, an emergency fund becomes your financial buoy, keeping you afloat during turbulent times. Let's elucidate how much you should earmark for emergencies and where you should store this fund.

**The Paramount Importance of an Emergency Fund**

Insulating yourself from financial shocks is critical to secure a financially stable retirement. The possibility of unforeseen expenses like sudden hospital bills, major car repairs, or an unexpected hike in your living expenses can become less daunting if you have a safety net to fall back on.

**Determining the Size of Your Emergency Fund**

A rule of thumb often advised by financial experts is to maintain an emergency fund sufficient to cover three to six months' worth of living expenses. However, this is not a one-size-fits-all equation. Your exact buffer should factor in your lifestyle, your financial obligations, and your tolerance for risk.

For instance, if you're financially supporting adult children or anticipate higher healthcare costs due to complex medical conditions, you may benefit from a more substantial safety cushion. Conversely, an investment portfolio that generates significant passive income, along with a frugal lifestyle, could necessitate a smaller emergency fund.

**AI's Role in Determining Your Emergency Buffer**

Artificial intelligence can assist in forecasting your potential future expenses based on your health, lifestyle choices, inflation, and market trends. At the same time, it takes into consideration your financial obligations and income sources, making the figure far more accurate and personalized than any manual estimates.

**Location of Your Emergency Fund**

Now let's address where you should store your emergency fund. This should ideally be an easily accessible, low risk, and liquid investment. Here are three potential places:

1. **High-Yield Savings Account:** These accounts offer an interest rate higher than the national average, ensuring your money continues to grow albeit at a conservative rate.

2. **Money Market Account:** This account combines the benefits of a savings and checking account, offering a relatively higher interest rate while allowing you some transactional privileges.

3. **Short-Term Certificates of Deposits:** CDs generally offer a higher interest rate than savings accounts. However, your money is locked away for a set time period, and early withdrawal can result in penalties. It's suitable for a portion of your emergency fund, but it's crucial not to lock away all your resources.

**AI Enhancing Your Emergency Fund Strategy**

AI and fintech have given rise to different robo-advisors and mobile apps designed to simplify the process of setting up and managing an emergency fund. From automatic deductions from your paycheck to optimization of the fund allocation across different assets for ideal balance, AI makes the process effortless and efficient.

As AI extends its reach into the very fabric of financial planning, it is revolutionizing the way we prepare for retirement, including how we set aside emergency funds. Predictive analysis and personalized recommendations have the potential to dispel the uncertainty surrounding retirement planning. Still, its successful implementation requires understanding its implications and strategic use.

# INVESTMENT APPROACHES IN THE AGE OF AI

## *Traditional vs. AI-Driven Investment Strategies*

Understanding the strengths and limitations of both traditional and AI-driven investment strategies is critical as we sail into uncharted waters of AI-dominated financial planning. So, let's elucidate the comparative landscape of traditional investment models to the bold new world of AI-enhanced investing.

**Understanding Traditional Investment Strategies**

Traditionally, investment strategies have relied on comprehensive financial analysis, in-depth market research, and the investor's risk tolerance and financial goals. Numerous investment philosophies have shaped the market over the years, with broad categories typically falling into two camps:

1. **Active Management:** This approach involves buying and selling securities to outperform certain benchmarks. Fund managers rely heavily on market research, trend analysis, and judgments about individual security selection.

2. **Passive Management:** This strategy involves duplicating a specific index or fund, aiming for long-term growth with reduced fees. It's based on the efficient market hypothesis, which asserts that stock prices reflect all relevant information, eliminating the chance of consistently 'beating' the market.

**The Advent of AI-Driven Investment Strategies**

AI and machine learning have begun redefining the investment landscape, demonstrating a potential to disrupt traditional investing as we know it. AI-driven strategies leverage voluminous data sets, machine learning, and predictive algorithms to unearth investment opportunities that could remain hidden in traditional models. AI tools can process and analyze huge amounts of data with speed and accuracy beyond human capabilities.

These AI systems can recognize patterns, trends, and relationships in the data, providing predictive insights and making investment decisions based on those predictions. They learn from historical data and then apply that learning to current and new data sets, fine-tuning their analysis and recommendations as they go.

**Comparing Traditional to AI-Driven Strategies: Strengths and Limitations**

Traditional investment strategies have a long history and a solid track record. These models rely heavily on human judgment, intuition, and experience which holds value especially when dealing with market anomalies and unusual circumstances. However, traditional models are limited by human cognitive biases and the inability to process vast data with speed and accuracy.

On the other hand, AI-driven investment takes advantage of the massive power of data processing, machine learning, and predictive analytics. These tools can operate around the clock, ceaselessly sifting through data points, devoid of any emotional influence for objective decision-making. Moreover, AI-driven strategies can capture non-linear patterns and high-dimensional interactions which are impossible to discern with traditional tools.

However, AI-driven models are not without limitations. They require vast, high-quality data sets to function accurately; the old adage "garbage in, garbage out" still applies. Plus, these algorithms can be black boxes, with the process of decision-making obscured, leading to transparency concerns.

As we stand on the brink of a transformative era in investing, embracing AI doesn't necessitate entirely deserting traditional modes of investment. An optimally designed AI-supported investment strategy would combine the strengths of both traditional and AI-driven models. Knowledge of the market from traditional models teamed with the machine efficiency and predictive capabilities of AI could revolutionize the investment scene, propelling us towards a future poised for unprecedented financial growth.

**How AI is Revolutionizing the Stock Market**

Artificial Intelligence (AI) has become a groundbreaking force in many sectors, but perhaps nowhere is its impact more profound than in the stock market. AI brings machine-learning capabilities, automation, and unprecedented precision to the intricate world of investment, significantly transforming the landscape. Here, we will explore the key ways AI is revolutionizing the stock market.

**Expediting Data Analysis**

AI's strength lies in its ability to rapidly and accurately process copious amounts of data that would be cumbersome and time-consuming for a human. The traditional approach often involves poring over reams of financial reports, sales figures, and similar data to make informed decisions. AI conquers these tasks swiftly, analyzing complex financial instruments, historical data, and current market trends within a fraction of the time a human would require, allowing for faster and more informed decision-making.

**Automated Trading**

Automated trading systems, or 'robo-advisors', are taking the financial world by storm. These AI-powered systems base their buying and selling decisions on a set of defined rules, making decisions at a pace unthinkable for human traders. The algorithms they utilize can rapidly analyze a wide range of variables such as price, timing, volume, and volatility, enabling real-time trading at a speed that gives it a competitive edge.

**Risk Management**

Risk management is a crucial aspect of investment, and AI is helping to redefine it. With AI, investors can proactively predict and manage uncertainties, making investment less a game of chance and more of a calculated science. Sophisticated machine learning algorithms consider multitudes of risk factors and their interrelationships, forecasting market volatility and aiding in developing risk-mitigation strategies. This also supports regulatory compliance since the systems can be set to operate within predefined boundaries.

**Predicting Trends**

AI and machine learning excel at identifying patterns and learning from them. They can sift through enormous data sets, highlighting patterns unseen by human eyes, and can also predict future trends based on historical data. This predictive capability is invaluable in stock market trading, where understanding and capitalizing on future trends can deliver significant financial advantage.

**Mitigating Human Bias**

Human emotions and cognitive biases can often lead to skewed decision-making in trading. Fear, greed, herd instinct, and overconfidence often lead to irrational decisions. However, AI-driven systems are devoid of emotion and immune to cognitive biases. They base their decisions purely on data and pre-defined rules, offering a degree of objectivity that human traders may struggle to uphold.

While the influence of AI on the stock market is undeniable and largely beneficial, it's not without its challenges. Issues such as data privacy, transparency of algorithms, and potential concentration of power raise valid concerns that warrant serious consideration. Despite this, AI's presence in the financial world is unlikely to wane; rather, as the technology advances, its impact will probably deepen.

In this evolving landscape, the key to making the most of AI's potential in the stock market will be in striking a balance: leveraging AI's strengths while understanding its limitations, using it as a tool to aid human decision-making rather than replace it. As we navigate the waters of this new era of AI-driven investing, those equipped with a mix of cutting-edge technology and a keen human intellect will be best prepared to make waves.

## The Future of Cryptocurrency and Blockchain in Retirement Planning

The integration of technology into finance has given rise to revolutionary concepts that are reshaping our understanding of monetary transactions, retirement planning being no exception. Cryptocurrency and blockchain technology have emerged as potentially transformative forces in this arena. Let's delve into their future implications and applications within retirement planning.

**Understanding Cryptocurrency and Blockchain**

Before exploring their role in retirement planning, let's define cryptocurrency and blockchain. Cryptocurrency is a type of digital or virtual currency that uses cryptography for security. Unlike traditional currencies issued by government bodies (fiat currencies), cryptocurrencies such as Bitcoin and Ethereum operate on decentralized platforms.

The backbone of these platforms is a heritage tech called blockchain - a distributed ledger technology that records transaction details across many computers, ensuring that the record cannot be altered retroactively, thus providing a high level of data integrity and security.

**Cryptocurrency and Retirement Portfolio Diversification**

In the world of retirement planning, diversification is king. The age-old wisdom of "not putting all your eggs in one basket" rings true, and cryptocurrencies are emerging as a new asset class to consider. They provide a new means of portfolio diversification that can potentially yield high returns over time.

Cryptocurrencies, due to their encrypted, decentralized nature, offer a level of protection against inflation – a critical consideration for long-term retirement planning. However, it's crucial to note that the crypto market's notoriously high volatility requires careful consideration and conservative allocation when including it in your retirement portfolio.

**Blockchain Technology and Retirement Planning**

Blockchain technology offers immense potential to streamline and enhance retirement planning processes. As a distributed, secure digital ledger, blockchain can store and track all transactions related to retirement plans providing immutable, transparent records.

Blockchain can also play a significant role in enhancing the portability of retirement plans. Traditional pension structures can complicate job transitions due to constraints in transferring retirement funds. A blockchain-based system can streamline the process, allowing for seamless transference of assets tracked through secure blockchain ledgers.

This technology can facilitate immediate, frictionless payments and the automation of certain operations, including claiming pensions, which becomes significant as we move towards a more globalized, digitally driven world.

**Cryptocurrency in Defined Contribution Plans**

There's increasing interest in including cryptocurrency in 401(k) plans or other defined contribution retirement plans. Companies like Bitwise Asset Management are developing cryptocurrency index funds – a concept similar to mutual funds – that may be included in tax-advantaged retirement accounts.

Additionally, certain Self-Directed Individual Retirement Accounts (SDIRAs) allow for cryptocurrency investments. Possessing the ability to invest IRA funds into crypto assets, SDIRAs offer investors a unique degree of flexibility in their retirement planning.

**Blockchain, Smart Contracts, and Annuities**

Looking ahead, blockchain could fundamentally reshape annuities and guaranteed-income products. Smart contracts – self-verifying, self-executing contracts transcribed into blockchain - are an innovative tool for managing annuities. By automating payouts based on predefined rules and without the need for intermediaries, smart contracts could reduce administrative costs, increase efficiency, and ensure precise, timely fulfilment of terms.

While cryptocurrencies and blockchain technology have the potential to enormously transform the landscape of retirement planning, they also come with new risks and challenges. Investors must navigate regulatory uncertainties, potential technological glitches, market volatility, and the relatively unknown long-term performance of these new assets.

These technologies are not a panacea, but they represent valuable new tools for individuals and advisors planning for retirement. Though in its early stages, the integration of cryptocurrency and blockchain into retirement planning is well underway, promising exciting possibilities for the future. The key will be in understanding their intricacies, effectively managing the risks, and integrating these tools wisely within a well-rounded, diversified retirement strategy.

# CHAPTER 5: SCOIAL AND PSYCHOLOGICAL IMPLICATIONS

## THE EMOTIONAL AND SOCIAL CHANGES OF RETIREMENT IN A TECH-DRIVEN WORLD

*The Psychological Impact of*

## *Early vs. Late Retirement*

The transition into retirement is one of life's most significant milestones, an event that profoundly impacts our lifestyle, identity, and psychological well-being. Intriguingly, your age at retirement can influence the type and degree of these impacts. This section will shed light on the psychological nuances of retiring early versus later in life, and guide you in preparing mentally for this new chapter.

**The Allure of Early Retirement**

The notion of early retirement often carries a romantic flair. It represents freedom from the daily grind, the opportunity to enjoy leisure time while still young and healthy enough to do so. However, jumping hastily into this appealing prospect could lead to unintended psychological repercussions.

On a positive note, early retirees can experience reduced stress related to work pressures, providing a sense of liberation and increased time to explore hobbies, travel, or invest time in relationships and communities.

However, early retirement also brings unique challenges. People who identify strongly with their careers may struggle with loss of professional identity, potentially leading to feelings of purposelessness and depression. This can be particularly pervasive among those who derive a significant sense of satisfaction and self-worth from their work.

Moreover, the sudden surplus of free time can be daunting. Without proper planning, retirees might find themselves aimless and bored, which can negatively impact mental health.

**The Impact of Later Retirement**

Retiring later in life, on the other hand, offers its own set of psychological implications. Delayed retirement can provide additional income and increased financial stability, which can significantly reduce stress and anxiety associated with financial security in retirement.

Additionally, extended engagement with work can stimulate cognitive activity, providing a sense of purpose and improving mental health. This continued sense of fulfillment, productivity, and social connectivity can be particularly beneficial in aging societies, where increased life expectancy outpaces the health-adjusted quality of life.

Nevertheless, working into older age may yield difficulties. Depending on the type of work, physical demands may become overwhelming, and workplace stress might take a heavier toll. Additionally, employees may face age-related biases, and struggle to keep pace with rapid technological advancements in their industries.

Furthermore, later retirees might potentially have less time to enjoy their golden years. Their health condition at retirement may not permit them to engage fully in activities they had planned, leading to feelings of regret or frustration.

**Planning for Psychological Well-being in Either Case**

Whether you choose to retire early or late, thorough preparation and mindful transition planning are critical for maintaining psychological health. Consider the following tips:

1) **Seek purpose beyond work:** Cultivate hobbies, interests, and social relationships that provide a sense of achievement and purpose independent of your job. This practice will help soften the blow of losing job-attached identity after retiring.

2) **Plan for your time:** Don't let the vast expanse of free time in retirement intimidate you. Develop a clear vision of what daily life in retirement will look like, and consider part-time work, volunteering, classes, or regular participation in hobby groups to provide schedule and structure.

3) **Physical health and mental health are connected:** Regardless of retirement age, regular exercise and proper physical health care are essential for maintaining mental health.

4) **Stay cognitively active:** Embrace lifelong learning. Intellectual stimulation can help preserve cognitive abilities, reduce the risk of dementia, and provide a sense of personal growth and satisfaction.

5) **Prepare financially:** No matter when you choose to retire, sound financial groundwork reduces anxiety and enables satisfying retirement experiences.

Early or late, retirement is a major life change that holds the promise of new freedoms and opportunities. However, undoubtedly, the shift also brings unique psychological challenges. Addressing these head-on and strategically planning for the mental impacts of retirement can make all the difference, turning this life stage into an invigorating journey of personal growth and enjoyment.

### Finding Purpose and Community in a Post-Work Life

The end of your working life does not signify the end of productive living. Yes, you might be bidding goodbye to long-standing routines, daily interactions and a concrete sense of purpose your work has offered for decades. However, retirement can be the window to a new universe of possibilities where you find rejuvenating meanings, renewed intentions, and a vibrant social community.

**Embracing the New Chapter**

To find your purpose in a post-work life, begin by adopting a positive mindset towards retirement. It is not a cessation of productivity, but the commencement of something novel and potentially even more fulfilling. Whether it's reigniting old hobbies, learning a new skill, embarking on travels that you've always dreamt of, or giving back to your community - there are umpteen avenues for self-discovery and purpose waiting to be explored.

**Finding Purpose through Passion and Talent**

Identify the things that truly captivate your interest. Always wanted to play the piano, paint landscapes, or dive into aquatic photography? Now is the time! Through hobbies and interests, you can inculcate a sense of daily structure, productivity, and satisfaction.

Remember, the goal is not to recreate the stress or rigor of your job but to seek an exercise that enriches your soul, keeps you mentally engaged, and optimizes your talents. It can be as simple as tending to your flower garden, pet sitting for your neighbors, writing a blog about your treasured recipes, or narrating nightly bedtime stories for your grandchildren.

**Volunteering and Mentorship: Giving Back to Community**

Volunteering can be an excellent avenue to find purpose in retirement. Helping at local food banks, teaching at a community center, involvement in conservation initiatives or spending time at an animal shelter not only allows you to contribute to society but also opens up opportunities for social interaction, thereby warding off feelings of isolation or loneliness.

Alternatively, consider mentorship. With the wealth of knowledge and experience you've gathered in your profession, mentoring young individuals in your field can be a rewarding and self-fulfilling exercise.

**Staying Socially Connected**

Retirement can disrupt your social life to some extent as workplace camaraderie is replaced with considerable solitude. However, it also offers ample scope to build new relationships or revive old connections neglected due to work pressures.

Participate in local community events, join clubs or groups (book clubs, hiking groups, music classes) that align with your interests, and invite new neighbors or old friends for coffee or a meal at your home. The digital revolution also allows you to stay connected with loved ones and friends living far away through video calls, social media, and virtual communities.

Building friendships in retirement is not just about filling your social calendar; it serves a higher purpose concerning companionship, shared experiences, emotional support, and lives enriched through diverse perspectives.

**Mindful Transitions**

Remember to be patient with yourself during this transition phase. The journey to a meaningful retirement will undoubtedly have its highs and lows, a few trial and error moments as you navigate your way through a major life transformation. Keep an open mind to new experiences, be patient with setbacks, and celebrate your progress.

Retirement is yours to define. This chapter of life offers an exceptional opportunity to re-write your life script, discover new territories of purpose, and build a tight-knit community that enriches your golden years. With the right mindset, lifelong learning, and social engagement, you can weave a thriving, meaningful, and joyous post-work life.

## Addressing the Isolation in an Increasingly Digital World

If there was one phrase to capture the tenor of our modern, technologically driven times, it would be 'hyperconnected yet alone.' We are living in an era where humans are more connected than ever, thanks to the Internet and the rise of social media. Yet, such connectivity has also caused an epidemic of loneliness. Retirees, who lack daily engagement with an active work community, can particularly feel this sting of isolation. Here, we take a look at how you can employ pragmatic strategies to stay engaged and overcome this sense of disconnect in an ever-increasing digital world.

**Understanding the Digital Divide**

Younger generations are often referred to as 'digital natives,' having grown up in the age of the internet. But for older adults, who are 'digital immigrants,' navigating through complex technology interfaces can be challenging. The tech-savvy communication platforms, although designed to bridge gaps, may inadvertently create a moat between you and your loved ones, pushing you further into isolation.

However, this digital divide is not a chasm that's impossible to traverse. With a willingness to learn and adapt, you can cross over this divide and leverage technology to tackle loneliness.

**Building Digital Proficiency**

Acquiring even the basic digital skills such as maintaining an email account, engaging on social media platforms, or getting the hang of video call applications can do wonders for your social connectivity. Start small and gradually expand your technological fluency. Use technology to stay in touch with family and friends, be a part of virtual communities, join online courses or workshops. The key lies in seeing the Internet not as an alienating hurdle, but as a conduit to meaningful connections.

**Embracing Virtual Communities**

The virtual world is bustling with plenty of active and welcoming communities. Online forums, groups, and clubs have mushroomed on various platforms that encompass a wide range of interests, from book clubs, movie discussion groups, gardening communities, fitness forums to DIY hobby clubs. Joining these can help keep that feeling of isolation at bay.

Remember, participating in these communities does not imply you have to be a passive consumer. Use this as an opportunity to share your wisdom, experiences, and learn from others in the community.

**Leveraging Technology for Emotional Wellbeing**

The rise of artificial intelligence (AI) is not only about automation and data science. It has profound implications for mental health too. Several AI-driven applications and tools are available today that can help in managing stress, anxiety, and boosting emotional well-being. From mood monitoring apps, mental health chatbots to online counseling platforms, AI indeed has a role in addressing the psychological impact of isolation.

**Staying Safe Online**

As you embrace digital platforms for engagement, it's crucial to be aware of online safety. Be vigilant about sharing personal information, understand privacy settings on social media platforms, and be wary of online scams.

**Digital Detoxification**

Even as we talk about digital engagement, it's important to strike a balance. Just as in-person social interaction can be draining for some, so can constant digital interaction. Carve out times in the day when you would disconnect from all digital devices. Spend that time for yourself – a walk in the park, meditation, or just soaking in the quiet can help rejuvenate you.

To sum up, the digital world can be a boon for retired individuals dealing with loneliness. Learning to use technology for communication, connection, and self-care can significantly enhance the quality of life in retirement. As you step into this digital arena, remember that patience and proactive learning are your best allies. Also, personal safety should always be paramount. As you construct your post-work life in this digital age, let technology serve as your bridge to meaningful interactions rather than a barrier.

# BUILDING MEANINGFUL CONNECTIONS AND MAINTAINING A SENSE OF PURPOSE POST-RETIREMENT

## *The Role of Social Platforms and Online Communities*

The explosion of social platforms and online communities has entirely rewritten the rules of social interaction. Today, these platforms offer retirees a unique opportunity to maintain active social lives, find like-minded individuals and counteract isolation without leaving the comfort of their homes. Here, we delve deeper into understanding the significance and benefits of engaging with social platforms and online communities in retirement life.

**Understanding the Power of Social Platforms**

Social platforms are digital infrastructures where people

from across the globe converge, exchange ideas, and build relationships. These platforms, such as Facebook, Twitter, LinkedIn, Instagram, and others, allow you to stay connected with not only friends and family but also engage with larger communities comprising individuals from diverse backgrounds and experiences.

From sharing photos of your gardening success on Instagram, connecting with former colleagues on LinkedIn, engaging in Facebook groups discussing your favorite books, or simply tweeting your thoughts out to the world, these platforms have plenty to offer for your post-retirement life.

**Benefits of Social Platforms for Retirees**

1. **Maintaining Relationships**: Social platforms make it easier to stay in touch with your family, old friends, colleagues, and acquaintances, aiding in the maintenance of relationships.

2. **Cultivating New Connections**: You can find and befriend like-minded individuals, engage in intellectually stimulating conversations, and even build a whole new community of friends online.

3. **Staying Updated**: Being on a social platform helps you stay abreast of the latest happenings in society, up-to-date information about your interests, and news around the world.

4. **Sharing and Expressing**: Social platforms also serve as spaces for self-expression. From sharing your wisdom, experiences, and opinions to exhibiting your hobbies and passions, they provide outlets to express your identity.

**Exploring Online Communities**

Online communities refer to a group of individuals connected through the internet based on shared interests, goals, or experiences. These communities exist on various platforms – from Facebook Groups, LinkedIn Groups, hobby forums, as well as platforms like Meetup that host multiple communities based on diverse interests.

Regardless of how niche your interest might be, there likely exists an online community for it. For a retiree, this is an excellent opportunity to dive deeper into your passions, connect with individuals who share them, and feel a sense of belonging.

**Benefits of Online Communities for Retirees**

1. **Shared Interests & Mutual Support**: Community members often share resources, advice, and support each other, contributing to an enriching learning environment as well as emotional support.

2. **Widening Horizons**: Engaging with diverse individuals in online communities helps widen your perspectives and exposes you to different viewpoints.

3. **Boosting Self-Esteem**: Contributing to these communities with your insights, experiences, or resources can give a sense of accomplishment and boosts self-esteem.

Navigating the world of social platforms and online communities requires some patience and the willingness to learn. However, the benefits far outweigh the initial challenges. As you explore these digital social landscapes, remember to exercise caution, respect privacy, and practice digital etiquette. Happy exploring, and here's to a connected, enriched retirement life!

**Volunteering and Mentorship Opportunities in the Age of AI**

As we embark on the AI age, numerous opportunities for volunteering and mentorship have emerged, particularly for retirees. The fusion of your years of professional and life experiences, coupled with a growing understanding of the AI landscape, can lead to profound impacts in both volunteering and as a mentor.

**Volunteering in the AI Era**

In the age of AI, volunteering has taken on new dimensions. Many not-for-profit organizations and educational institutions are seeking individuals with knowledge and experience to help them navigate the complexities of artificial intelligence. Volunteering in such capacities not only provides a sense of purpose but can significantly contribute to society's betterment.

1. **Educational Initiatives**: Many organizations focus on educating youth about AI and its implications. As a retiree, your understanding and wisdom can be harnessed to help cultivate future generations' knowledge.

2. **Non-profit Support**: Non-profit organizations are always in need of extra hands. Your understanding of AI can boost their operational competence, help them leverage AI capabilities, and improve their efficiency.

3. **Community Outreach**: As AI permeates everyday life, there's a growing need to help local communities understand and adapt to these changes. Volunteering your time to raise awareness, dispel misconceptions about AI, and train

individuals in new technology use can have a massive impact.

**Mentorship in the AI Era**

Mentorship has always held a significant place in professional fields, and this continues in the AI era.

1. **Industry Mentoring**: Professionals entering the AI field often require mentorship to navigate the burgeoning and complex field. Giving back by mentoring such individuals can be immensely satisfying and beneficial for the field's growth.

2. **Inter-generational Mentorship**: The AI era has exacerbated the partisan divide between different generations in terms of technology usage. As mentors, retirees can guide the elderly in understanding and embracing AI fundamentals, bridging the technology gap to create an inclusive future.

3. **Entrepreneurial Mentorship**: The AI era has spurred a wave of new entrepreneurs. Your industry insight and an understanding of AI can prove invaluable to newcomer entrepreneurs navigating the AI integration in their ventures.

The transition from a conventional workforce to a world increasingly dominated by AI can seem daunting. Still, retirees have an unparalleled opportunity and the potential to leverage their wisdom, professional insights, and new-found understanding of AI to profoundly impact individuals, organizations, and communities.

By embracing the roles of both volunteers and mentors, retirees can contribute to shaping a future where AI is not a force of disruption but rather an instrument of evolution, progress, and unity. The age of AI, therefore, offers the remarkable possibility to not merely navigate your retirement but make a valuable contribution during it.

## Lifelong Learning and Pursuing Passions in the Age of AI

In the context of retirement, the phrase 'lifelong learning' morphs from being a trite catchphrase into a literal necessity, accentuated in the AI era. With technology reframing the world at a relentless pace, keeping updated on current trends can keep you engaged, mentally agile, and socially connected. By coupling this learning journey with the pursuit of passions you've nurtured, retirement can transform into a fulfilling and enriching stage of life.

**Lifelong Learning in the Age of AI**

Learning, in the context of the AI age, transcends beyond traditional classrooms. Here are compelling reasons and ways to adopt lifelong learning as you navigate retirement in the AI era:

1. **Understand the AI Landscape**: The AI evolution isn't reserved solely for the technical world. From smartphones to smart homes, AI has nestled itself into everyday life. Gaining a rudimentary understanding of AI can demystify its workings and allow you to harness its power more effectively.

2. **Stay Socially Connected**: As digital platforms become the mainstay for interaction, embracing technological learning can help retain your social connections, combat isolation and foster new relationships.

3. **Develop New Skills**: An array of online learning platforms currently offer courses on virtually every subject imaginable, many of these focusing on AI and technology. Engaging with

these can open vistas for new abilities and competencies.

4. **Promote Cognitive Health**: Research has increasingly indicated that continuous learning can have positive effects on cognitive health, keeping your brain fit and flexible.

**Pursuing Passions in the Age of AI**

Retirement unfurls an expanse of time to deeply invest in your passions. In combination with the opportunities that AI presents, it can be an excellent conduit to both realize and fuel your interests:

1. **Hobbies in the AI Age**: AI has revolutionized previous hobby areas. Be it photography, where AI aids in optimizing images, or gardening, where AI can monitor plant health, understanding AI can lend an exciting edge to your hobbies.

2. **Exploring New Areas**: If you're eager to delve into new interests, AI presents a world of possibilities. For example, you could explore digital art, try your hand at coding, or even learn how AI works.

3. **Bridge Learning and Passion**: AI can bridge the gap between learning and passion. With AI technologies, you could learn a new language, master a musical instrument, or even comprehend complex concepts with augmented realty.

In all, lifelong learning in the AI era is not merely about keeping pace with technology but about amplifying the quality of life during retirement. By aligning this with the pursuit of passions, the AI era can indeed turn retirement into a vibrant, challenging, and gratifying journey. Rather than viewing the prospect of retirement in the AI era as unsettling, you can look at it as an exciting challenge - a second innings, laden with opportunities for growth, exploration, and contentment.

# ADDRESSING THE POTENTIAL FOR INCREASED NEUROTICISM AND ANXIETY

## *The Psychological Toll of Financial Uncertainties in the AI Era*

Life, by virtue of being unexpected, holds within it the seeds of uncertainty. Financial volatility, one of life's most taxing uncertainties, can cast long shadows over the golden years of retirement, more so in the constantly evolving landscape of AI. Exploring the psychological implications of financial uncertainties and identifying coping strategies is a crucial step towards creating a cushioned, confident and healthy retirement journey in this AI-defined epoch.

**The Psychological Strains of Financial Uncertainties**

1) **Anxiety and Stress**: Financial concerns are among the leading causes of stress, which if left unchecked can cascade into anxiety disorders. As constant companions of uncertainty,

anxiety and stress not only lead to mental health disorders, but they can also influence physical health, contributing to ailments such as hypertension, heart disease, and sleep disorders.

2) **Depression**: Prolonged financial worries can often lead to feelings of hopelessness and a resulting state of depression. In retirement, where social interactions might already be pared down, these feelings can become magnified and further exacerbating the situation.

3) **Cognitive Impact**: Chronic stress, particularly related to financial worries, can impair cognitive functions over time, inhibiting your ability to process information and make rational decisions — further augmenting the spiral of financial uncertainty.

**Coping Strategies and Resilience-Building Techniques**

Preparation and a proactive approach are key in managing financial uncertainties and their resultant psychological impact:

1) **Education and Understanding**: Knowledge is power. A robust understanding of financial principles coupled with keeping abreast of AI trends can go a long way in dispelling fears and uncertainties. Financial literacy can help you navigate unpredictable financial terrains, and furthermore, empowerment via understanding can alleviate associated psychological strains.

2) **Professional Guidance**: As the landscape of retirement planning broadens with technological advancements, seeking professional aid becomes increasingly important. Financial advisors, particularly those skilled in navigating AI developments, can offer valuable guidance and help demystify

the complexities of retirement planning.

3) **Embracing Technology**: AI offers a wealth of tools designed to simplify financial planning. Leveraging these instruments can help minimize uncertainties and build a comprehensive and flexible retirement blueprint.

4) **Stress Management Techniques**: Regular physical exercise, meditation, mind-body relaxation techniques, and maintaining a healthy lifestyle serve as strong antidotes to stress and anxiety related to financial uncertainties.

5) **Community Support**: Join community groups, online forums, or enrol in courses with like-minded individuals navigating the same phase in life. Such gathering of minds can be a source of peer advice, moral support, and often, novel solutions to shared concerns.

Financial uncertainties are an inherent part of life's journey, and more so, an unwelcome amendment to the retirement narrative in the modern era. By acknowledging the potential psychological effects of these uncertainties, and arming oneself with the right tools, knowledge, and mindset, it is possible to navigate the uncharted waters of financial planning in an AI-dominated landscape with confidence and peace of mind. The retirement period, rather than becoming a constant battle with financial worries, can then more peacefully morph into an enriching and enjoyable chapter of life.

**Techniques and Strategies for Managing Stress and Anxiety in the Era of AI**

We are living in an age where the changing nature of work, the economy and retirement structures are undergoing seismic shifts. The forces driving these changes are rooted in the relentless march of AI and technology. In this new landscape, stress and anxiety can be constant companions, and managing them efficiently is important for both psychological and physical well-being. Combating these psychological adversaries effectively involves a balanced mix of cognitive strategies, lifestyle changes, and the thoughtful application of AI itself.

**Cognitive Techniques**

1) **Mindfulness**: Rooted in ancient wisdom, mindfulness is the practice of staying in the present moment. It means observing and accepting thoughts and feelings without judgement. By adopting mindfulness, we can alleviate anxieties about uncertainties, including retirement and AI shifts, and manage stress more coherently.

2) **Cognitive Behavioral Therapy (CBT)**: This is a structured form of therapy that helps identify negative patterns of thought, evaluate their validity, and replace them with healthier thoughts. Through CBT, you can learn to manage anxiety triggers, including financial uncertainties and AI-induced changes.

3) **Positive Affirmations and Visualization**: Positive affirmations involve repeating positive sentences to oneself, thereby boosting morale and will. Visualization involves picturing a state where the desired outcome has been achieved. These techniques can subdue anxiety and instil a sense of control.

**Lifestyle Modifications**

1) **Exercise**: Regular physical activity boosts endorphin levels,

known as 'feel-good' hormones, which can elevate mood and act as natural stress reducers. Activities suggestive of moderate intensity, like brisk walking, swimming, or even dancing, can counter stress and anxiety effectively.

2) **Nutrition**: A balanced diet rich in fruits, vegetables, lean proteins, and whole grains can boost your mood, provide energy, and reduce symptoms of stress and anxiety.

3) **Sleep**: Adequate rest is important to manage stress and anxiety. AI developments have led to the invention of numerous sleep-tech devices and apps that can help monitor and enhance your sleep patterns, helping you feel refreshed and better equipped to handle stressors.

4) **Social Connections**: Fostering strong connections with friends, family and a wider community provides an emotional buffer against stress. In today's digital age, even when physical meetings are not always possible, AI-backed social platforms can help in maintaining these vital connections.

**Leveraging AI for Stress and Anxiety Management**

AI technology itself is changing the face of stress and anxiety management. AI-driven apps and devices can provide personalized techniques for stress management. These include guided meditations, sleep improvement aids, and AI-powered therapy platforms. However, it's crucial to remember that while these tools can be helpful, they should not replace professional help when needed.

By integrating cognitive techniques, lifestyle modifications and leveraging AI, one can combat and control stress and anxiety triggers, thereby ensuring a smoother and more enjoyable transition to the new retirement paradigm in an AI-driven future. Not only is managing this crucial for your retirement years but also an integral part of day-to-day life, helpful in creating an overall balance amidst flux and uncertainty.

## Embracing Change and the Importance of Mental Wellness

In this rapidly changing world, the arrival of AI continues to redefine our understanding of work life, retirement, and the future. Embracing change becomes an inherent requirement, not just a choice. This shift not only disrupts traditional norms but also forces us to re-evaluate our mental wellness strategies while addressing anxieties about change.

**Understanding the Landscape of Change**

A key component in embracing change is understanding the changing landscape. AI, automation, and digital transformations are ushering in a new era of opportunities. Understanding these changes helps greatly in the process of acceptance and can alleviate the stresses associated with fear. Recognize that change is constant, and further, that it opens up doors to novel experiences and prospects.

**Adopting a Growth Mindset**

In dealing with massive changes like the advent of AI, adopting a growth mindset becomes indispensable. A growth mindset, a term coined by psychologist Carol Dweck, is characterized by the belief that abilities and intelligence can develop with time and practice. This mindset not only equips us to handle uncertainties better but also fuels our capacity for lifelong learning, curiosity, and resilience.

**Role of Lifelong Learning**

Being open to learn and adapt is a critical factor in embracing change and maintaining mental wellness. Many assume learning ends with formal education, but in fact, learning should be a never-ending process. Be it AI-related skills or any new technology, openness to acquiring new knowledge not only secures one's place in the changing workforce but also affirms self-confidence and reduces anxieties related to change.

**Embracing Failure**

The AI era might force us to step outside our comfort zones and take risks. In such scenarios, failure may be an inherent aspect. It's important to view failures as stepping stones to learning, as opposed to setbacks. Embracing failure helps foster resilience and alleviates stress associated with fear of failure.

**Prioritizing Mental Wellness**

Prioritizing mental wellness is vital during times of change. This means acknowledging your feelings during these uncertain times, and seeking professional help when needed. Proactive steps, such as stress management techniques, mindfulness, regular physical activity, maintaining a balanced diet, and socializing are valuable approaches for sustaining mental health. AI-driven solutions such as health tracking devices and platforms offering therapy services can also be noteworthy allies in maintaining mental wellness.

Ultimately, the future world with proliferating AI might seem daunting, but by understanding the changing landscape, adopting a growth mindset, embracing lifelong learning, accepting failures, and prioritizing mental wellness, we can navigate into the future with optimism and resilience. Indeed, embracing change and prioritizing mental wellness is not just beneficial but absolutely crucial in today's unfolding scenario. It forms a cornerstone of not just successful retirement in an AI-driven world, but a more balanced and fulfilled life in general.

# CHAPTER 6: THE ENTREPRENEURIAL SPIRIT IN RETIREMENT

# HARNESSING THE OPPORTUNITIES PRESENTED BY AI

## *Identifying AI-driven business opportunities*

The advent of Artificial Intelligence presents a trove of exciting business opportunities. These span across a myriad of sectors, leveraging AI technology for increased efficiencies, better customer service, improved analytics, and many more. Identifying these opportunities--particularly those aligning with existing skills, experiences, or passions--can be a transformative step towards securing financial stability in the AI era.

**Understanding AI and its Potential**

Artificial Intelligence can appear complex, but understanding its basic workings demystifies its potentials and opens up myriad possibilities. AI's core strength lies in its ability to learn from data, make decisions, and continuously improve. It's already driving change in industries as diverse as healthcare, finance, retail, and logistics, making processes smarter and more efficient. Understanding these changes underscores the vast possibilities AI brings for business.

**Exploring Different AI Opportunities**

Several niches within the AI world offer profitable business opportunities. Here are few avenues to explore:

- AI Consultancy: With AI being an essential part of businesses, an AI consultant can play a vital role. They can guide businesses to integrate AI into their processes and strategies, helping them drive efficiency and profits. If you possess expertise in AI and a knack for understanding business needs, this pathway could be ideal.

- AI-Driven Data Analytics: Businesses thrive on data and insights. Offering services to help organizations decipher complex data and gain actionable insights through AI-powered data analytics can unlock huge business opportunities.

- AI Hardware: Specialized hardware that supports AI operations, like machine learning and deep learning chipsets, is in high demand. Entering the manufacturing or distribution of AI processors can be profitable if you have a background in hardware technologies.

- AI in Healthcare: From patient data analysis to predicting illness risks, AI in healthcare offers myriad opportunities. Developing AI applications that assist in healthcare provision can hold immense potential.

- AI in Education: AI can personalize learning like never before. If education and technology are your passions, leveraging AI to offer personalized, inclusive learning solutions can offer substantial business opportunities.

**Market Research**

Before committing to any business opportunity, thorough market research should be prioritized. Understanding the competition, the consumer needs, latest trends, and potential growth rates, is critical to establishing a successful venture. Employing AI analytics for market research could provide more profound insights.

**Building a Network**

Networking with AI professionals, business strategists, and attending relevant AI or entrepreneur gatherings can help in grasping the technological and business aspects of AI. This network can open pathways to partnership possibilities, mentorship, investment opportunities, and future clients.

**Launching a Business**

Once an opportunity is identified and sufficient research is conducted, developing a business plan and launching your endeavor is the final step. While running a business does come with risks, it also potentially holds significant rewards in the rapidly advancing AI era.

Just as with the advent of the internet, which completely transformed the business landscape, AI is poised to do the same. Identifying and capitalizing on AI-driven opportunities today could pay off exponentially tomorrow, paving the way for a successful business, meaningfully contributing to society, and offering financial security to embrace retirement with confidence.

## Tips for Launching a Startup in Retirement

Retirement, a phase associated traditionally with slowing down, offers an opportunity to embrace new beginnings. The advent of technology, especially Artificial Intelligence (AI), provides a wealth of untapped entrepreneurial prospects. As a retiree, launching a startup allows you not only to keep your skills sharp and stay mentally active but also to secure financial independence. This section aims to offer comprehensive advice on how to navigate the challenges of launching a startup in retirement.

**(a) Leverage Your Experience**

Drawing on years of accumulated wisdom, professional experience, and industry knowledge is beneficial when starting a new venture. Your professional insights will serve as a competitive edge and can be instrumental in identifying gaps in the market.

**(b) Define Your Vision and Mission**

Begin your entrepreneurial journey by defining your vision. Clearly outline what you aspire to achieve with your startup and how you plan to make this a reality. Your mission will serve as the guiding force of your venture.

**(c) Cultivate a Robust Business Plan**

Whether seeking funding or approaching potential business partners, a well-rounded business plan plays a critical role in showcasing the viability of your startup idea. It should be comprehensive, including details about your target market demographics, budget forecasts, revenue sources, marketing strategies, and business goals.

**(d) Investigation and Market Research**

Understanding your competitors and customers is essential for business success. Conduct thorough research to identify market trends, recognize consumer needs and preferences, and comprehend competitor strategies. In today's digital age, employing AI data analytics tools can offer salient insights.

**(e) Embrace Lifelong Learning**

As an entrepreneur in the AI-era, it will be beneficial to keep learning. Whether it's about AI technology, regulatory developments in your industry, or digital marketing strategies, staying up-to-date is essential to adapt and thrive in the dynamic business landscape.

**(f) Build a Supportive Team**

Running a startup can be daunting. Surrounding yourself with a team of motivated, skilled, and dedicated individuals will ease the journey. It's also key to remember that team members can be both young and experienced individuals. The synergy of fresh ideas and seasoned experience can propel your startup ahead.

**(g) Establish a Strong Online Presence**

In the AI era, having a strong online presence is a non-negotiable aspect of running any successful business. From an interactive website to engaging social media platforms, your online presence is a tool to reach and interact with your target audience, build your brand, and increase visibility.

**(h) Networking and Mentorship**

Building connections with industry professionals, networking at relevant events, and seeking mentorship can expedite your startup's growth. They can provide priceless guidance, potential partnerships, and opportunities for attracting investments.

**(i) Lean into Passion**

Finally, ensure that your business idea is something you are passionate about. Starting a business in retirement gives you the luxury of choosing something you love to do. Passion will fuel your venture, make the journey enjoyable, and drive you to commit in the face of challenges.

In the dynamic landscape of entrepreneurship, retirement could be the opportune moment to begin a new venture. Your professional experience when combined with passion and resilience can lead to the successful launch of an AI-driven startup, granting not just financial security but also personal fulfillment in your golden years.

## Building a Brand in the Digital Age

Marketing and branding have always been intrinsic to the success of any business. In the digital age, with the advent of AI and the rise of social media, building a brand is no longer a privilege restricted to large corporations. As a retiree looking to launch a startup, you find yourself in an era of immense opportunities to carve your unique brand identity. Whether it's a brand rooted in years of professional expertise, a passion project turned business venture, or the latest AI-enhanced service, this section will guide you in constructing your brand in the digital age.

**(a) Recognize the Power of Branding**

Branding is vital. It differentiates your business from the competition, creates a recognizable identity and builds customer loyalty. Your aim should be to establish a brand that resonates with your target audience and manifests the essence of your offerings.

**(b) Define Your Brand Persona**

Every brand has a persona - a distinctive identity that defines its nature and character. This persona should be aligned with your target market's preferences. Analyze your audience, their needs, aspirations and the traits they appreciate to create an appropriate brand persona.

**(c) Digital Footprint**

Your digital footprint plays a defining role in building your brand. From your official website to your social media profiles, ensure every element is aligned with your brand persona. Your online presence should be robust, engaging and consistent, serving as an easy touch point for your potential customers.

**(d) Leveraging AI in Branding**

AI can be an invaluable asset in your branding journey. AI-driven tools can analyze customer behavior, feedback, reviews, and trends to provide detailed insights. This information assists in refining your branding strategy, understanding your customer's needs better and creating highly targeted marketing campaigns.

**(e) Value-driven Content**

Creating value-driven, relevant content is key to establishing your brand's credibility. This can take several forms - insightful blog posts, informative videos, engaging infographics. According to your customer's preferences, adopt a suitable content strategy which educates, informs, and adds value providing a steady stream of traffic to your site.

**(f) Social Media**

Platforms like Facebook, LinkedIn, Instagram, Twitter, and others offer a great channel to reach out, interact, and engage with your audience on a personal level. Regularly posting content related to your business, responding to comments, engaging in discussions will accumulate interest and followers, thus amplifying your brand recognition.

**(g) Building Relationships**

A successful brand is built on meaningful relationships with customers. Be approachable and responsive, whether it's a customer's query, review, or complaint. This not only creates happy and loyal customers but also enhances the reputation of your brand.

**(h) Consistent Branding**

Maintaining consistency in your branding efforts is integral. Keep the tone of your communications, visual elements, brand values consistent across various channels.

**(i) Measure, Learn, Adapt**

Utilizing AI-powered Analytics tools can quantify the impact of your efforts, providing a clear picture of your brand's performance. Learning from this data and adapting your strategy accordingly will accelerate the growth of your brand.

Building a brand in the digital age, though challenging, can be remarkably rewarding. Leveraging digital tools effectively and consistently will assist in developing a brand that resonates with your audience, ultimately leading to a successful venture that thrives in the transforming business landscape.

55)Inspiring stories of retirees-turned-entrepreneurs:

**55) Inspiring Stories of Retirees-Turned-Entrepreneurs**

At an age where many contemplate a laid-back life, there are some fearless retirees who choose to dive into the adrenaline-packed world of entrepreneurship. They apply their vast storehouse of knowledge, experience, and wisdom to build successful ventures. These inspiring stories of retirees-turned-entrepreneurs are a powerful testament to the fact that age is just a number, and passion knows no boundaries.

**(a) The Story of Bob's Red Mill Natural Foods**

Among these inspiring tales is the story of Bob Moore, the founder of Bob's Red Mill Natural Foods. After retiring from his jobs in the tech industry, Moore developed a passion for old-world milling techniques. He turned this passion into a business at 50, which has now become a multi-million dollar natural food company. Moore's story shows how indulging one's curiosity and passion can lead to entrepreneurial success, irrespective of age.

**(b) The Journey of Colonel Sanders and KFC**

One of the most globally recognized retirees-turned-entrepreneurs is Colonel Harland Sanders, the founder of Kentucky Fried Chicken (KFC). At the age of 65, when most would enjoy the ease of retirement, Sanders found himself penniless and decided to utilize his cooking expertise. His passion for fried chicken and his unique recipe led to the establishment of one of the world's largest fast-food chains. This highlights that it's never too late to turn things around.

**(c) The Success of Jimmy and Dee Haslam with Pilot Flying J**

After retiring from their previous occupations, Jimmy and Dee Haslam took over Jimmy's father's petrol business, Pilot Flying J, at ages 68 and 62 respectively. Today, it stands as North America's largest operator of travel centers and truck stop, showing the importance of grit, perseverance, and effective leadership.

**(d) The Story of Radiant RFID Founded by Cynthia and Kenny Ratton**

Cynthia and Kenny Ratton, both in their 50s, decided to invest their retirement savings into a startup, Radiant RFID. Today, it counts many major corporations and government agencies among its clients. This story encourages seizing opportunities that align with current technological trends and the importance of risk-taking.

**(e) John Goodenough's Vital Contribution to Technology**

At an age when most have long since retired, John Goodenough invented the lithium-ion battery at the age of 57, revolutionizing portable electronic devices. Decades later, at 94, he developed the first all-solid-state battery cells, further demonstrating that creative contribution to technology has no age limit.

These stories of retirees-turned-entrepreneurs illustrate the transformative power of passion, perseverance, and adaptability in overcoming obstacles and achieving entrepreneurial success. They further underline that retirement can be a launchpad, rather than a finish line, providing a new lease of life through entrepreneurship. Whether it is converting a hobby into a business or keeping up with modern technology, these stories inspire retirees to dream, achieve, and contribute uniquely to the ever-evolving entrepreneurial landscape. Hence, remember, it's never too late to start. It's always too early to cease.

**The Health Benefits of Staying Active and Engaged**

Regardless of one's age, a critical ingredient for a balanced and fulfilling life is staying active and engaged. This is especially true during retirement when individuals often have more free time at their disposal. Staying mentally, physically, and socially active offers numerous health benefits.

**(a) Mental Benefits**

Engaging in intellectually stimulating activities promotes mental health by keeping the brain active and sharp. Retirement offers the ideal time to learn new skills or rekindle old interests. Pursuing hobbies and engaging in pursuits like reading, writing, artistic activities, playing musical instruments, or learning a new language are wonderful ways of maintaining cognitive vitality. Studies show that mental agility helps in delaying cognitive decline and potentially reducing the risk of dementia and Alzheimer's disease.

**(b) Physical Benefits**

Besides mental engagement, physical activity is a vital aspect of maintaining health during retirement. Being active helps reduce the risk of conditions such as stroke, coronary heart disease, type-2 diabetes, and even some cancers. Regular exercise helps regulate body weight, lowers blood pressure, and improves overall mobility and strength. It also slows down the aging process. Even simple activities like gardening or regular walks are step towards staying physically active.

**(c) Social Engagement**

Feeling connected is an essential aspect of human existence. Staying socially engaged can significantly improve quality of life, reduce feelings of loneliness, and improve mental well-being. It also boosts cardiovascular health and increases longevity. Participating in community events, engaging in volunteer works, joining clubs, or even staying connected with friends and family online can enrich social engagement.

**(d) Psychological Well-being**

Engaging in meaningful activities provides a sense of purpose and enhances self-esteem. It leads to greater contentment and life satisfaction. Moreover, continuing to learn and grow contributes to a positive outlook on life and increases psychological resilience. It gives a feeling of accomplishment and boosts overall happiness and well-being. In addition, giving back to society through volunteering offers a profound sense of fulfillment and purpose.

**(e) Longevity and Quality of Life**

Active and engaged life is closely linked to longevity and improved quality of life. The regular mental, physical, and social stimulation affirmatively impacts overall health and well-being, contributing to a longer lifespan. Moreover, continuously learning and staying connected gives joy, optimism, and motivation, thereby enhancing the quality of life.

On reflection, retirement is not about slowing down but changing gears. So, whether it's starting a business, learning a new skill, or simply spending more time outdoors with people or nature, staying active and engaged redefines the retirement landscape. Embrace this rewarding journey of discovery that keeps you vibrant, healthy, and alive at every stage of life - and indeed, your golden years can indeed be your best years!

## Finding and Cultivating New Passions

Retirement ushers in a phase of life when one has the luxury of time and freedom. It serves as a gateway to the unexplored territories of interests, hobbies, or passions that might have been shelved due to occupational constraints. Finding and nurturing new passions are significant aspects of living a fulfilling retired life.

**(a) The Joy of Discovery**

Within each person rests a wellspring of untapped potential and undiscovered passion. Expanding one's horizon by learning new things and engaging in different activities initiates the joy of discovery. Be it mastering a foreign language, picking up a musical instrument you have never played, diving into a complex book, dabbling in cooking or gardening, or even exploring the intricacies of chess, the possibilities are limitless. The retirement years provide the perfect opportunity to embark on a journey of exploration and learning that not only enhances one's knowledge but also provides a sense of accomplishment.

**(b) Health and Wellness**

Cultivating a new passion can also be a route to better health. For instance, regularly practicing yoga, learning to dance, or taking up running can positively impact physical health. On a flipside, hobbies like painting, reading, writing, or crafting are known to encourage mindfulness, reduce stress levels, and positively influence mental health. Engaging in activities you love provides a therapeutic effect, promoting overall well-being.

**(c) Building and Strengthening Social Connections**

Life after retirement may result in fewer social interactions, leading to a sense of isolation. However, finding and cultivating new passions can open gates to new social arenas. Joining clubs or online communities revolving around shared interests can foster a sense of belonging and combat loneliness. New connections can contribute to mutual learning and sharing, leading to enriched experiences.

**(d) Cultivating Self-Expression**

Nurturing a new passion can serve as a powerful mode of self-expression. Taking up sketching or painting can open an avenue for unleashing creativity. Writing poetry or stories can be a channel to express emotions and share experiences. Pursuing passions allows you to express your unique personality and experience the joy of creativity.

**(e) Enhancing Self-Esteem and Confidence**

Mastering new skills and excelling in a hobby naturally fuel self-esteem and confidence. Cultivating new passions challenge you, stretching your boundaries and capabilities. Every step forward and every small victory in this journey helps you understand your worth better, empowering you with enhanced self-confidence.

In summary, retirement is not the end; instead, it is a beautiful beginning to a new chapter of life. It is an opportunity to explore, learn, grow, and above all, enjoy the process of finding and nurturing new passions. This journey of self-discovery and self-fulfillment adds sparkle to the golden years, making retirement truly enchanting.

# Stories of retirees who found success post-retirement.

**Real-world examples of flourishing second careers**

(A) Introduction

The golden age of retirement often comes with a sense of renewal, offering fresh opportunities to explore and venture into previously unchartered waters. A number of retirees have leveraged this phase to kickstart second careers, proving that age is no bar to learning, growing, and achieving success. Let's delve into some inspiring real-world examples of individuals who, after significant careers, found renewed purpose, passion and prosperity in second careers post-retirement.

(B) From Teacher to Tech-Entrepreneur

One such inspiring tale is of Bill Zipp, a retired high school teacher from Portland, Oregon. After spending decades in the education sector, Bill explored the growing field of technology and founded an app development company, at the age of 65. His app, which aids in managing savings and expenditure for retirees, has found considerable success in the smartphone-savvy senior community, transforming him into a tech-entrepreneur.

(C) From Corporate Executive to Bestselling Author

Another remarkable second-career story is of Mary Lawson. After spending 30 years as a corporate executive, she retired only to start a career as a novelist in her late 60s. She leveraged her wealth of life and professional experiences into compelling narratives. Her debut novel, written on the cusp of retirement, climbed its way to the bestseller list, marking the beginning of prolific second innings as a writer.

(D) From Accountant to Café Owner

Singapore's Lim Bee Huat provides another insightful example. Huat, a long-time accountant, had cherished the vision of opening a unique café that serves specialty local coffee. The post-retirement phase bestowed him with the time and resources to turn this dream into reality. Today, his café is renowned citywide for its delightful brew and inviting ambiance, offering him an active, fulfilling, and profitable second career.

(E) From Engineer to Environmental Activist

Finally, we have the tale of Tsering Norbu, a retired civil engineer from northern India who became an environmental activist in his golden years. Disturbed by the deteriorating environmental status of his hometown, Leh, Norbu launched a volunteering group comprising of other retirees. They work passionately to clean and protect the region's natural beauty, demonstrating how a thriving second career can also contribute to society's welfare.

The one common thread running through these different stories is the people's courage to explore uncharted territories, their determination to learn and adapt, and the relentless pursuit of their dreams. These inspiring tales of flourishing second careers instill the belief that age is just a number when it comes to creating impact and achieving success. As we move forward in the AI era, plenty of such opportunities will continue to bloom, providing retirees a chance to redefine their second innings with zeal and zest. Embrace the possibilities; your best career might just be waiting around the corner in your golden years.

**Lessons learned from their journeys**

(A) Introduction

The stories of successful second careers express myriad learnings, displaying a testament to the multifarious journeys that shape meaningful retirements. These experiences provide valuable lessons for those contemplating their own post-retirement paths. Below is an exploration into the consequential takeaways from the remarkable journeys of these retirees-turned-entrepreneurs.

(B) Embrace Change and Lifelong Learning

Bill Zipp's transformation from a high school teacher to a tech entrepreneur underscores the importance of embracing change and committing to lifelong learning. With growing advancements in technology, new opportunities to engage and innovate can emerge even in the most classical sectors, such as teaching. It is crucial to remain flexible and adaptive, evolving with the changing market trends and consumer behavior.

(C) Leverage Previous Work and Life Experiences

Mary Lawson's successful plunge into novel writing after a thriving career as a corporate executive exemplifies the potential of harnessing previous work and life experiences. Any profession or industry develops a rich amalgamation of skills and experiences, which can serve as vital assets in launching a second career. The art lies in recognizing these transferrable skills and capitalizing on them.

(D) Pursue Unfulfilled Dreams and Passions

Lim Bee Huat's journey from being an accountant to a café owner underscores the golden opportunity retirement provides to pursue unfulfilled dreams and passions. Having a clarity of vision and the courage to actualize it can turn into a rewarding endeavor, both financially and personally. Financial stability gained through the initial career often provides the necessary resources to explore these ventures.

(E) Contribute Positively to the Society

Tsering Norbu's shift from civil engineer to environmental activist foregrounds another inspiring lesson: the valuable potential of retirees to contribute positively towards society. Many individuals possess the desire to work towards societal well-being, but are often constrained by work pressures and responsibilities. Retirement can lead to the freedom needed to actualize these aspirations, shaping your second career around causes you are passionate about.

The above insights drawn from these stories provide a glimpse into the possibilities that retirement can bring, helping individuals chalk out their messages for the future. As AI continues to shape various industries and sectors, the lines demarcating retirement and work are continually blurred. The future of retirement could indeed be a gateway to new opportunities, more learning, and even grander successes. Prepare to reimagine retirements in this intimate dance with AI, for the golden years can indeed be the most active, engaging, and fulfilling.

# CHAPTER 7: ETHICAL CONSIDERATIONS IN THE AI AGE

# THE IMPLICATIONS OF AI DECISION-MAKING IN RETIREMENT PLANNING

*Advice for those looking to follow a similar path*

(A) Introduction

Treading the path of retirement can be as daunting, if not more, than the journey of starting a new career. Against the backdrop of rapid technological change and a shift towards an AI-led economy, crafting a retirement that is fulfilling and financially secure can seem to be an overwhelming task. However, insights garnered from retirees-turned-entrepreneurs can help illuminate the roadmap for those seeking a fulfilling post-retirement career. Here's some advice forged from their stories:

(B) Embrace the New and the Unfamiliar

Navigating the terrain of an unfamiliar industry or pursuing an unexplored passion can be intimidating, but it is the first step towards personal and professional growth. Harness the power of curiosity and let it be your guiding force. Like Bill Zipp, who embraced the rapid progression of technology to transform himself from a high school teacher to a tech entrepreneur, be willing to explore and learn from new experiences.

(C) Build On Your Past Experiences

Draft the blueprint of your post-retirement career drawn from the rich experiences of your past work. Let the skills garnered and lessons learned guide your decisions, just as Mary Lawson did when she successfully transitioned from corporate executive to novel writer. Identify and leverage the knowledge and insights you've earned over years of work experience in creating your second career.

(D) Follow Your Dreams with Financial Prudence

Retirement provides the perfect space to unfurl the wings of your unfulfilled dreams. Like Lim Bee Huat, who waved farewell to his accounting career to passionately embrace the world of coffee, you too can chase your latent dreams. But do remember to balance passion with financial prudence. Draft a fiscal plan before venturing into a new business, and consider seeking professional financial advice to stay secure.

(E) Use Your Freedom for a Greater Cause

Retirement often provides the freedom from time constraints and work commitments. This newfound liberty, if utilized effectively, can contribute much to societal good. Just as Tsering Norbu's transition from civil engineer to environmental activist demonstrated, there is ample room for positive societal contributions in retirement. Yet, it's important to ensure the cause chosen aligns with your inner values and passion.

(F) Continually Adapt and Learn

Lastly, irrespective of the path you intend to tread in retirement, be prepared to continually adapt, evolve, and learn. As the world steers into an AI-led economy, the ability to learn and grow with changing trends will determine your success. Engage in lifelong learning, keeping pace with the evolving sector trends.

Retirement is not about retreating from an active life but rather redefining what that active life can look like. With AI rapidly revolutionizing industries and economies, our understanding of retirement must evolve. The second careers of retirees spotlight the ample opportunities that exist beyond traditional work, as the golden years can indeed, be the most fulfilling. So strap on and prepare for this exciting journey. As they say, life begins at the end of your comfort zone – may this be true for your golden years too.

**The debate over human vs. AI decision-making prowess**

(A) Introduction

In today's age, the implications of Artificial Intelligence (AI) on our daily lives and decisions are so profound that it has triggered a global discourse - the debate over the supremacy of human intelligence versus its artificial counterpart in decision-making. This discourse assumes heightened importance in the realm of retirement planning where well-informed and accurate decisions have far-reaching implications on one's financial security and overall well-being.

(B) The Rise of AI Decision-Making

Burgeoning advancements in AI have made it a crucial part of our financial planning ecosystem. Algorithms make complex calculations in microseconds, taking into account a multitude of factors. Robo-advisors, for instance, leverage AI to provide cost-effective and customized investment advice. An International Data Corporation (IDC) forecast estimates that by 2022, almost $6.2 billion will be funneled into robo-advisory services. On the surface, it seems as if AI is the panacea for all retirement planning woes. But is AI genuinely superior to human judgment?

(C) The Power of Human Decision-Making

Despite AI's rapid advancements, our innate human capacity for complex thought, emotional understanding, ethical considerations, intuition, and learned experiences cannot be understated. Human judgement brings with it a nuanced understanding and an ability to grasp context, emotion, and subtlety. David Grau Sr., in his book "Buying, Selling, and Valuing Financial Practices", spoke about the essential role financial advisors play in assuaging the fears and concerns of their clients - a task AI is yet to master. Humans can also comprehend abstract concepts such as trust and responsibility, things a machine would struggle to mimic.

(D) Merging the Strengths of AI and Human Intelligence

Rather than choosing between human intelligence and AI, what if we could bring together the strengths of both? The ideal future of retirement planning could be a hybrid model: human advisors utilising AI tools to enhance their decision-making capabilities. This "cyborg" approach combines AI's data processing capabilities with humans' critical thinking and emotional intelligence to create a robust decision-making structure. Instead of surrendering all control to AI, it becomes a powerful tool, augmenting human advisors' ability to make sound decisions and provide personalized financial advice.

(E) The Road Ahead

In conclusion, while AI's capabilities in decision-making continue to grow, complementing it with human intelligence seems to be the best path forward, especially in the delicate field of retirement planning. Decisions here need careful deliberation, require managing emotional transitions, and call for ensuring financial security while upholding ethical responsibilities. By harmonizing human intelligence with AI, we bring the best of both worlds together, helping individuals plan a secure, fulfilling, and well-managed retirement.

As we continue to examine and embrace the role of AI in retirement planning, fostering a deep understanding of the unique strengths and limitations of both human and artificial intelligence will only prove more crucial. It's our collective responsibility to shape this amalgamation consciously and carefully, with an eye towards a future that values and integrates both.

## Understanding algorithmic biases and potential pitfalls

(A) Introduction

The influence and advantages of Artificial Intelligence (AI) in retirement planning are undeniable. However, just like any other technology, AI is not infallible and is prone to inherent biases and potential pitfalls. One of the core topics sparking interest in the discussion around AI is the aspect of algorithmic bias. As we increasingly turn towards AI for resolving complex financial matters, understanding this bias becomes critical.

(B) Algorithmic Bias: An Overview

The concept of 'Algorithmic Bias' refers to systematic and repeatable errors in a computer system that create unfair outcomes, such as privileging one arbitrary group of users over others. Simply put, if the data fed into AI systems reflects a biased perspective, the output will inevitably mirror these biases. This can be problematic in retirement planning, where algorithmic biases might result in exclusionary, incorrect, or unfair financial advice.

(C) Examples of Algorithmic Bias: A Look at Real-World Cases

One controversial example of algorithmic bias is seen in the Apple Card credit limit scandal. In 2019, the algorithm responsible for determining credit limits came under scrutiny when notable tech entrepreneur David Heinemeier Hansson highlighted that his Apple Card credit limit was 20 times higher than his wife's, despite their shared assets and his wife's superior credit score. This incident raised questions about the potential gender bias concealed in the algorithm's decision-making process.

In the world of retirement planning and financial advice, such biases can have serious implications - the wrong advice can significantly impact a retiree's financial security.

(D) The Underlying Causes and Potential Pitfalls

Algorithmic biases stem primarily from biased data, flawed design, or discriminatory feedback loops. If an AI tool has been fed historical financial data that reflect societal biases - such as gender or racial wage gaps - the tool will likely perpetuate these biases.

AI tools that rely on algorithms can also be led astray by 'noise' or irrelevant data leading to erratic and unpredictable consequences. Take the world of investing for instance, where AI-driven investment strategies could become overly complex or opaque, and passionate amateur investors - or even professional traders - may find them difficult to understand, leading to potential catastrophic losses.

(E) The Way Forward: Addressing Algorithmic Bias

Recognising and addressing algorithmic bias early on holds the key. Rigorous testing, bias audits, increased transparency in algorithms, and diversification of development teams can help mitigate these biases. Encouraging regulation and legislation to hold AI systems and their creators accountable can also play a pivotal role.

As we employ AI in the sensitive realm of retirement planning, it is imperative to remember that AI is a tool - one that we need to design, refine, and regulate thoughtfully. Algorithmic biases underline the need to remain cautious and informed about the potential pitfalls concealed in embracing AI blindly. The focus must remain on harnessing AI's potential while diligently rectifying its weaknesses, turning it into a reliable ally for those entering the golden years of retirement.

## Ethical considerations in data usage and privacy

## (A) Introduction

An essential component of the AI-enhanced world is its heavy reliance on data. Data is now regarded as an essential resource, as pivotal to an AI system's functioning as oil is to the engine of a car. However, alongside this dependence on data echoes the echoes of a critical ethical debate - the matter of data usage and privacy.

## (B) Ethical Dilemmas Around Data Usage

In the realm of AI-driven retirement planning tools, data usage necessitates a fine balancing act. On one hand, AI systems need extensive data to function effectively and provide personalized financial advice. On the other hand, these requirements must not override the ethical and legal rights of people to their personal information.

Additionally, there's also the ethical concern over who controls and owns the data. For instance, if a retiree's data contributes to the AI's learning and subsequently its success, should they benefit directly from it?

## (C) Privacy Concerns: Implications for Retirees

Privacy concerns are equally paramount. Although AI-driven retirement tools can offer unprecedented personalization in retirement planning, it also implies that these technologies end up knowing a lot about the retirees— their income patterns, spending habits, and lifestyle choices.

Given the sensitive nature of such information, privacy infringement can have serious consequences. In the hands of unethical individuals or organizations, such information can be misused for identity theft or financial frauds, devastating the retiree's financial standing.

(D) Data Misuse: Real-World Instances and Consequences

Examples of such concerns aren't just hypothetical. The infamous Cambridge Analytica scandal underscored the chilling implications of data misuse. The firm was accused of harvesting personal data from Facebook users without consent to influence voting behavior. This incident served as a stark reminder of the consequences when data privacy is breached.

(E) Mitigating Ethical Concerns: The Role of Regulations and Transparency

Policies and regulations have a crucial role in mitigating these concerns. General Data Protection Regulation (GDPR) in the European Union, for instance, has set a precedent in ensuring stricter control and consent mechanisms over personal data.

Along with stringent regulations, companies must also focus on improving transparency regarding data usage and privacy policies. Often, these policies are buried in complex legal language, making it hard for users to understand the extent of data they're parting with.

While AI offers promising advancements in the realm of retirement planning, it's equally important to navigate the ethical landscape mindfully. Understanding and addressing the ethical implications around data usage and privacy is not just a regulatory requirement but also a moral obligation.

Businesses and policymakers together must champion forth to create a balance between personalization and privacy, ensuring that AI serves as a tool for good that retirees can trust with their futures. Privacy should not be the price paid for progress and personalization, and as we march forward into a technologically advanced era, we must keep this ethical compass in mind.

## Recognizing and addressing inherent biases in AI systems

(A) Introduction

An exciting facet of AI systems is their impressive ability to learn, adapt, and evolve through machine learning algorithms and extensive datasets. However, alongside this laudable transformative potential, exists the disconcerting reality of inbuilt biases. These inherent prejudices within AI systems, especially in those driving retirement planning solutions, can be profoundly damaging if left unaddressed.

(B) Understanding AI Biases: Source and Consequences

The biases manifest in AI systems are typically the result of skewed or incomplete data they're trained on. If the dataset used to train an AI system lacks diversity or perpetuates existing inequalities, certain social groups may be inadvertently disadvantaged.

In the context of retirement planning, such AI bias could inadvertently lead to financially disadvantageous advice for certain demographics, perhaps favoring particular investment strategies that might not be beneficial for everyone.

(C) Real-World Instances of AI Biases

Examples of AI bias are not hard to find. For instance, an AI developed by Amazon for hiring purposes had to be scrapped as it showed a bias against resumes from women. It had learned this bias from the historical data that women are less likely to be hired in Amazon.

In another instance, a research study found that an algorithm used in the US healthcare system was less likely to refer black people than white people who were equally sick to programs that aim to improve care for patients with complex medical needs.

(D) Addressing AI Biases: Mitigation Strategies

Recognizing the potential harm of AI bias, it's critical to undertake measures to mitigate them actively. This mitigation begins with ensuring that the AI is trained with quality diversified data that reflects the different aspects of society.

Transparency in AI systems is another critical mitigation strategy. AI's decision-making processes should be transparent and explainable. It should not be a 'black box' and should be able to explain why it is making certain decisions.

Regular auditing of AI systems can further help identify and correct bias. Experts or third-party organizations can conduct these audits, ensuring the system continues to learn and evolve without inherent prejudices.

(E) The Role of Regulations in Preventing AI Biases

Policymakers also have a critical role in formulating regulations to prevent AI bias. This role extends beyond merely prescribing rules but also ensuring their strict adherence. Govt. also need to instill regulatory bodies to oversee the implementation and monitoring of these regulations.

While AI's transformative potential can dramatically improve retirement planning, the inherent biases within these systems cannot be ignored. Mitigation strategies and robust regulations are of paramount importance to ensure AI serves as an equitable and reliable tool.

As we navigate through this exciting yet challenging landscape, it's essential to remain committed to the principles of fairness, transparency, and inclusivity, ensuring that no retiree is left disadvantaged in the wake of AI's breakthroughs.

## Ensuring transparency in AI-driven retirement tools

(A) Introduction

Having discussed the inherent biases prevalent in AI systems, it is now imperative to delve into the importance of transparency in AI-driven retirement tools. This transparency not only ensures an equitable approach to retirement planning but also instills faith in the users of these tools regarding the data-driven decisions made on their behalf.

(B) Defining Transparency in AI

So, what do we mean by transparency in the context of AI? Essentially, transparency pertains to the explainability of an AI system. It delineates the ability of a user to understand

and trace the decision-making process of the machine. This understanding empowers users to validate, trust, and fully leverage the recommendations and decisions put forth by the AI-enabled retirement tools.

(C) Why Transparency Matters

One may question - why does transparency in AI matter? To begin with, it holds the key to deciphering if the AI system has learned and implemented the right solution. This transparency also fosters trust, helping clients to better comprehend and thus, confidently accept the AI's decision. Specifically, in the domain of personal finance and retirement planning, this understanding is of utmost importance, given the sensitive nature of the decisions involved.

(D) Ensuring Transparency in AI

Several strategies can be adopted to ensure transparency in AI. Firstly, it is crucial that the machine learning models used are interpretable by nature. For example, linear regression models are easier to understand and explain. It is also essential to develop and implement AI in a 'white box' approach, indicating that every step of the processing is open and visible.

Additionally, AI systems should be equipped with 'interpretability methods' that can provide insights into how they make decisions. For instance, a tool called Local Interpretable Model-Agnostic Explanations (LIME) can be used to explain the predictions of any classifier, thus promoting transparency.

(E) The Role of Legislation and Regulation

Governments and regulatory bodies have a massive role to play in ensuring transparency in AI systems. Implementing stringent regulations can ensure that companies are constrained to develop AI which is transparent.

The EU's General Data Protection Regulation (GDPR) is one such statutory law ensuring the right to explanation where automated decisions are involved.

(F) Conclusion: Balancing Transparency with Competency

On a concluding note, while pursuing AI transparency, it is necessary to strike the right balance between transparency and competency. Over-explaining every single decision can hamper efficiency and usability. As we tread this path of innovation, it is about creating the right balance and fostering an environment where AI can help us plan our retirements confidently and transparently.

The future of AI-enhanced retirement planning should not be an enigma but a transparent, understandable tool for bettering our golden years.

## Advocating for a retirees' bill of rights in the age of AI

(A) Introduction

On the road to ensuring the beneficial interplay of AI and retirement planning, one key facet is the establishment of a retirees' bill of rights. Our focus in this new age of AI must be to ensure the fair and equitable treatment of retirees. To do so, a bill of rights specifically oriented towards retirees, dealing with their rights, privileges, and protections in this rapidly digitising landscape, is warranted.

(B) Why a Retirees' Bill of Rights?

The advent of AI and digital technologies has presented a risky yet rewarding landscape, especially for retirees grappling with the nuances of novel retirement planning tools. This age bracket, often wary of novelty due to inherent vulnerabilities, demands certain assurances. The financial and socio-emotional stability, that a retiree seeks, can be fostered by establishing a robust framework of regulations and policies designed to protect them.

(C) Key Components of the Retirees' Bill of Rights

Crafting a Retirees' Bill of Rights in the age of AI should consider several factors. It should encompass the right to transparency, the right to control individual data, the right to reliable and reasonably understandable financial advice, and the right to redress in case of grievances.

The Bill should also clearly define the role of AI advisors, ensuring that recommendations provided are in the best interests of the retirees, over and above the interests of corporations or financial institutions.

It must additionally have a provision for the education of retirees making the transition into this new age of AI-driven financial planning. This will help them optimise these platforms, ensuring they are equipped to use and understand these AI tools effectively.

(D) Implementation and Enforcement

Government and international regulatory bodies should take the lead in implementing and enforcing this Bill of Rights. They must continuously revise and adapt it in response to the evolving AI landscape.

Furthermore, penalties must be enforced for companies violating these rights. This would not only deter unethical practices but also encourage the development of technology that respects and advances the interests and rights of retirees.

(E) Conclusion: Towards a Fair AI-Driven Future

As we move amidst the tides of digital transformation, the retiree population shouldn't be sidelined in the discourse. Their unique needs and vulnerabilities must be respected and addressed in adaptations of AI tools and services.

A Retirees' Bill of Rights in the Age of AI would underline their importance in our fast-evolving society, ensuring that they are valued, protected, and benefitted in this new landscape. This would set a benchmark for equitable and ethical design and application of AI in the realm of retirement planning. With collaborative efforts from policymakers, technology designers, and society at large, AI can indeed revolutionize retirement, leading us towards a future that is secure, ethical, and fair for all.

# ADVOCATING FOR TRANSPARENT AND ETHICAL AI DEVELOPMENT

*The role of regulations and oversight bodies*

(A) Introduction

The formidable growth of AI-imbued technologies in the financial sector necessitates the establishment of robust regulatory mechanisms. Trustworthy AI transcends the creation of efficient systems. It necessitates safeguarding individuals' rights and fostering public good, where its relevance is especially eminent in the retirement landscape.

(B) The Need for Regulation and Oversight

The inherent complexity of AI makes comprehension and scrutiny challenging, even for the well-versed. This complexity, coupled with the potential risks of information manipulation and unsolicited data usage, calls for a well-defined regulatory framework.

The adoption of regulation in AI applications mitigates the risks of potential misuse and ensures efficient handling of ethical dilemmas. It also ascertains fair usage, protecting the interests of retirees, and ensuring that they are not victimized due to a lack of understanding or manipulation.

(C) Key Responsibilities of Regulatory and Oversight Bodies

Regulatory bodies must be entrusted to monitor firms that employ AI for financial activities, especially retirement planning and management. Providers of AI advisory services should be mandated to disclose the mechanics of their AI advisory algorithms and data handling practices, bolstering transparency.

The role of oversight bodies should extend beyond mere regulations. They need to ensure retirees are not only protected from inadvertent bias and manipulation, but also understand how to use AI retirement planning tools optimally. Education and frequent communication should be taken up, ensuring that the benefits of AI in financial planning extend beyond improved efficiencies and into improved consumer utility and comprehension.

(D) Collaborative Approach: Collective Responsibility

The structuring of regulatory and oversight mechanisms cannot be a unilateral process. Policy-makers, AI developers, industry experts, and society all have important roles to play. A collaborative dialogue among these stakeholders would serve to identify potential policy blind spots and garner diverse perspectives.

(E) Encouragement of Open Source AI

Oversight bodies should advocate for free accessibility and public scrutiny of AI systems. This open-source AI culture would encourage the development of secure and trustworthy systems while providing an opportunity for continuous refinement and improvement.

(F) Conclusion: A Structural Approach to Guard Trust and Ethics

An assertive approach to AI regulation does not stifle innovation, instead, it propels forward an ethical and trustworthy adoption of AI technologies. Oversight bodies play a crucial gear in this machinery of trust, with their defined roles promoting fair and balanced AI technologies, guaranteeing retiree rights, and instilling public confidence in an increasingly AI-dependent financial landscape.

As we push to the future with AI, the guiding hand of regulation and oversight would serve to shape a world where AI innovations foster societal good, safeguarding retiree interests and heightening their execution in the retirement planning landscape. Ultimately, regulation and oversight are not just integral aspects of the AI landscape, but pivotal in shaping the future of retirement in the AI age.

## Promoting open-source AI solutions for public scrutiny

(A) Embracing the Open-Source Ethos in AI

In the digital age, particularly in the field of artificial intelligence, the concept of open-source can serve as an effective tool in democratizing accessibility and fostering intellectual collaboration. Open-source AI solutions have the potential to empower users, from professionals to retirees, to evaluate, scrutinize, and enhance these technologies while maintaining transparency and accountability.

Embracing open-source models for AI in retirement planning would ensure these tools are accessible, understandable, and, above all, open to public scrutiny. It is a powerful means to allow direct engagement, promoting transparency, and facilitating continuous iterative development.

(B) Advantages of Open-Source AI Solutions

The open-source AI endeavor has the power to democratize AI development, allowing interested individuals and communities to access and contribute to algorithms that matter to their lives. In the retirement planning context, this could mean providing the public the means to validate technology vendors' claims about their AI, fostering trust and credibility.

More than just accountability, open-source models stimulate continuous learning and innovation. They allow various contributors to bring in interesting perspectives, therefore increasing the chances of discovering novel use-cases, identifying bugs, and improving system performance – all crucial factors in driving AI advancements in retirement planning.

(C) Ensuring Transparency and Trust

The trust element is critical when dealing with people's retirement plans and finances. Retirement is a sensitive stage of life, where decisions can severely impact a person's future financial security. Open-source AI platforms make the process transparent, putting people in a better position to trust these AI systems with their retirement planning.

(D) The Role of Regulatory Bodies

Regulatory bodies can encourage AI providers to adopt open-source models for their retirement planning platforms. Doing so would involve setting certain protocols as to what degree AI systems should disclose their algorithmic workings, balancing transparency with the necessary protections for intellectual property.

To foster open-source AI development, regulatory bodies need to ensure that these platforms are not just about publishing algorithms, but also about providing adequate documentation and interfaces for people to use and understand these platforms effectively.

(E) The Future of Open-Source AI in Retirement

The future of retirement planning in the AI age could see a blend of proprietary systems and open source platforms co-existing, providing retirees with a variety of options according to their needs and skill levels. It's crucial, however, that the advantages of open-source solutions are communicated clearly to the public. As more users involve themselves in open-source contributions, the AI industry stands to benefit from enhanced innovation, collaboration, and trust-building, ensuring retirement planning tools become more effective and accessible to everyone.

Open-source AI, if appropriately promoted and managed, promises to be a potent tool in the democratization of AI technologies. It can usher in ethical trustworthiness, public faith, and innovative enhancements, solidifying its place in the stitchwork of future AI-driven retirement planning.

## Building a future where AI serves humanity ethically

(A) Living in Harmony with AI

The integration of artificial intelligence into our lives is an inescapable evolution. From self-driving cars to personalized movie recommendations, AI has found its way into virtually every aspect of our day-to-day lives. As AI applications become increasingly ubiquitous, their ethical implications deserve careful scrutiny. Amid this shift, the ultimate goal must be a future where AI serves humanity ethically, upholding principles of fairness, transparency, and respect for user autonomy.

In the context of retirement planning, the ethical use of AI implies developing tools and solutions that ensure the financial security and well-being of retirees, while respecting their privacy and individual preferences.

(B) Principles of Ethical AI

Ethical AI is a broad philosophy that encompasses multiple components. Firstly, it requires an emphasis on transparency. This entails the openness of AI functions – allowing users to see and understand the decision-making processes within AI. Secondly, fairness is critical. AI must not discriminate on any grounds and ought to provide equal opportunities for all users. Thirdly, AI's respect for privacy. Sensitive information, like one's retirement plans and finances, should be thoroughly protected.

Finally, ethical AI applications should empower individuals, not suppress them. From providing tailored, insightful financial advice to recognizing and adapting to personal financial situations and goals, AI in retirement planning should be used as an empowering tool that enables retirees to make knowledgeable decisions about their future.

(C) Ethical AI: A Collaborative Endeavour

Building a future where AI serves humanity ethically cannot be a solitary pursuit. It requires the cooperation of multiple stakeholders – from developers, users, and government bodies to academic scholars and ethicists. Policy and law play an influential role in shaping these ethical norms. Rules and regulations ought to be implemented to ensure AI respects privacy, treats all users fairly, and employs transparent algorithms.

Public input is a crucial part of this process. The future of AI should be decided democratically, with all society members voicing their goals and concerns. As AI becomes more integrated with our lives, public literacy about AI technology should be promoted to ensure informed decision-making about its adoption and use.

(D) The Future of Ethical AI in Retirement Planning

The future of AI in retirement planning holds immense potential, provided ethical considerations are properly addressed. Ethical AI can transform the retirement planning process into a personalized, precise, and user-friendly endeavor, significantly enhancing financial outcomes and security for retirees.

For instance, AI could leverage data analytics to offer customized financial advice, based on a retiree's individual financial goals and risk-tolerance levels. By engaging with various financial scenarios presented by AI, retirees could better understand their own financial standings and comfortably make informed financial decisions.

Tools that ensure the privacy and security of personal financial data will be crucial. Equally important would be the development of AI systems that continuously learn and adapt to evolving user preferences, market trends, and economic contexts. This flexibility would ensure constantly optimized retirement plans that are both realistic and maximally beneficial.

In conclusion, building a future where AI serves humanity ethically is an aspirational and attainable goal. It requires collective determination, effective regulation and a continual commitment to uphold the principles of fairness, transparency, and respect for autonomy. By adopting this targeted approach, the future of AI in retirement planning can be both ethically sound and tremendously liberating, promising retirees a secure, fruitful post-work life.

# CONCLUSION

# EMBRACING THE FUTURE WITH OPTIMISM AND PREPARATION

*The harmonious blend of AI with human ingenuity*

(A) Embracing the Blend

In the evolving landscape of technology, an ongoing synergistic relationship is being forged between Artificial Intelligence (AI) and human ingenuity. This partnership, combining AI's data-crunching prowess with the qualitative understanding and intuitive capabilities of humans, is set to revolutionise various aspects of life, including retirement planning.

The undeniable value that this harmonious blend brings to the table serves to ample up the potential of both facets. The seamless integration and mutual amplification lead to a co-creative force that pushes the boundaries of what is possible in the realms of financial management and retirement planning.

(B) Unleashing the Power of AI

The information age has generated a wealth of data. The analysis of this data and the extraction of meaningful insights is where AI shines. AI's ability to analyze vast amounts of data, discern patterns, and make accurate predictions is unparalleled.

In the context of retirement planning, AI tools can help sift through a sea of investment options, analyze market trends, and output effective strategies that can optimize future financial security. All this, however, is only half of the equation.

(C) The Human Touch

While AI's decision-making capabilities are becoming progressively competent, human ingenuity remains pivotal. Our inherent abilities to empathize, relate, and understand qualitative facets can advantageously drive the strategic use of AI.

Retirement planning, after all, isn't just about number-crunching. It involves deeply personal considerations, future dreams, risk comfort levels, and lifestyle aspirations which AI, as of now, cannot fully grasp. Here is where human input becomes particularly essential, adding the human touch to AI operations.

(D) Nurturing the Symbiosis

Ultimately, the best outcomes in the realm of retirement planning are likely to emerge from a balanced and harmonious relationship between AI and human insight. For example, while AI can tailor a retirement plan based on statistical analysis and pattern detection, humans can fine-tune it to ensure alignment with retiree values, emotional comfort, and long-term aspirations.

In addition, fostering an environment of continuous learning and adaptability is key. As AI systems grow and evolve, so too should our understanding and approach towards utilizing these tools. Embracing an attitude of lifelong learning will ensure we stay ahead of the curve and harness the benefits of this AI-human synergy.

(E) The Future Holds Promise

The harmonious blend of AI and human ingenuity paints a promising future for retirement planning. With AI as a powerful analytic tool and humans providing intuitive insights and personal understanding, retirees can look forward to comprehensive and tailored approaches that significantly heighten the potential for a secure, fulfilling retirement.

Such an innovative approach prompts us not just to adapt to technological changes, but also to influence them, ensuring they serve to enhance our financial well-being in the upcoming years. By tapping into this powerful AI-human synergy, we as a society can embark on a journey towards a financial future that is not only secure but also ripe with possibilities.

**The power of adaptability and resilience**

(A) Embracing Adaptability

In an era marked by rapid advancements in AI and technology, adaptability emerges as a crucial trait for successful retirement planning. The ability to adapt implies the capacity to accept new situations and adjust one's thought processes and actions accordingly.

This fluidity is especially relevant considering the dynamic nature of the technology sector. Each new day brings with it fresh developments, newer applications of AI, and consequently, several fresh challenges and opportunities. The nature of adaptability is such that it empowers individuals to be at the forefront of these changes, steering their impact positively on retirement planning.

(B) Resilience: The Backbone of Long-Term Success

Alongside adaptability, another significant attribute that comes into play is resilience. By definition, resilience represents our capacity to bounce back from setbacks, persist through difficulty, and forge ahead in the face of adversity.

In the context of retirement planning, resilience can take on several forms. It could be the ability to regain financial footing after a market downturn, the tenacity to keep learning new technological tools for financial planning, or the emotional strength to keep striving for financial security despite multiple setbacks.

(C) Adaptability and Resilience in Action

Practical application of these traits may involve consistently updating one's knowledge and staying informed about the latest AI tools available for financial planning and wealth management. It also implies learning and growing from past financial mistakes or market downturns.

On a larger scale, adaptability and resilience might mean

reinventing career roles to stay relevant in an AI-driven job market, or diversifying income sources to prepare for a future of vibrant gig economies.

(D) The Interplay Between Adaptability and Resilience

As we look at these two virtues side by side, it becomes evident that adaptability and resilience are mutually reinforcing. Adapting to changes often requires a degree of resilience, and similarly, being resilient generally requires an adaptable mindset.

Individuals who can adapt to the AI revolution's changes, and remain resilient in the face of its challenges, will likely navigate their path to retirement more successfully. This dynamic duo of traits serves as a powerful force to harness, enhancing one's ability to build a secure and fulfilling retirement in the AI era.

(E) Fortifying Adaptability and Resilience: The Road Ahead

Cultivating these traits goes beyond merely understanding their importance. It includes seeking out resources, adopting a growth mindset, and continually challenging oneself to step out of the comfort zone.

The power of adaptability and resilience in this age of AI offers an optimistic narrative for retirement planning. Embracing these traits can enable individuals to navigate technological advancements and unforeseen hurdles, paving the way for a secure, flexible retirement strategy that stands the test of time.

**Fostering a collective spirit of collaboration and trust**

(A) The Power of Collaboration

The march of progress in the AI era is unstoppable. But an individual's journey into this future should not be a solitary one. Collaboration plays a key role in the effective navigation of this terrain, particularly in retirement planning.

Collaboration translates into sharing knowledge, experience, and resources. Whether it's learning about AI-driven financial tools from a technologically-inclined friend, or pooling together resources with peers to invest in an AI startup, the collaborative approach can help mitigate risks and spread opportunities.

(B) Trust in the Digital Age

Trust, a concept as old as human society itself, assumes a different nuance in the digital age. Can AI be trusted? What safeguards are in place? How secure is the data being fed into these algorithms?

To answer these questions, one must consider the safeguards in place - the regulatory frameworks and legislation developed to keep AI systems in check. Though still in its nascent stages, efforts are underway globally to ensure transparency in AI operations, maintain data privacy, and ensure ethical AI decision-making.

(C) Collaboration and Trust within AI Systems

Amalgamating collaboration with trust, AI systems can act as enablers. With the power of machine learning, these systems can learn from the collective experiences of many, thereby offering insights into better retirement planning that a single person might miss.

At the same time, these systems can build trust by keeping data secure, delivering consistently accurate results, and demonstrating accountability in operations—resulting in an environment where AI is viewed as a trusted collaborator for the individual.

(D) Building Collaboration and Trust with AI

Being open to collaboration and fostering trust with AI goes hand in hand with knowledge and education. Stay informed about the latest trends and developments in AI technology. Understand the data privacy laws and how they protect you. Engage with communities, both offline and online, that focus on AI developments.

(E) Collaboration and Trust: Paving The Way to the Future

By fostering a spirit of collaboration and trust, we can tackle the evolving landscape more efficiently, pool intellectual resources to grapple with new AI trends, and establish a sense of community in a world that's becoming increasingly digitized.

A collective approach encourages information sharing, idea generation, and mutual support. Trust ensures that we can work with technology, not against or in spite of it. Together, they create a supportive and enabled environment that empowers us all to look ahead to the future of retirement with confidence.

Fortifying these elements, we can ensure not just individual success in retirement planning, but also foster a future where AI serves the larger good of society - ethically, transparently, and inclusively.

### Lifelong learning in a rapidly evolving landscape

Living in an era fueled by rapid technological advancements, it's only logical that to stay afloat, one needs to continuously adapt and learn. The cruciality of lifelong learning has never been more emphasized. With the accelerated rate of change in job markets due to AI and automation, revising skills and embracing new areas of knowledge is no longer a choice—it's a necessity.

When we think of lifelong learning, we usually relate it to climbing the career ladder or keeping up with industry trends. However, this also applies to retirement planning. As the landscape of financial management undergoes a seismic shift due to technology, grasping new financial tools, understanding economic trends, and adapting to evolving retirement paradigms will prove essential.

There's good news though - learning has changed, and not just for the younger generation. With the proliferation of digital platforms, learning has become more accessible, flexible and versatile. You can learn almost anything online, at your own pace and in the comfort of your home. Whether it's a new AI tool, understanding blockchain technology, or getting to grips with economic trends - the digital landscape offers endless learning opportunities.

Specifically, in the realm of AI, being aware of what AI can offer and its limitation will enable wiser decision-making in retirement planning. Understanding how your data is used, what 'machine learning' actually means, or how one AI tool differs from another can contribute significantly to crafting that flawless retirement plan.

Creating a culture of learning involves seeking out knowledge, expanding your skill set, and keeping an open mind to new concepts. It involves stepping out of comfort zones, embracing the belief that it's never too late to learn, and putting what you learn into action. This belief is the core of a learning culture.

Infusing lifelong learning into retirement planning doesn't just enhance your financial perspective—it plays a crucial role in fostering personal growth, delaying cognitive aging, and enhancing social networking opportunities.

Embracing ongoing education prepares us for the constantly evolving economic landscape and the uncertainty of AI revolutionary impacts. It enables us to take control of our financial destiny, empowers us with the autonomy to navigate our choices and helps us create a robust retirement plan crafty enough to withstand the vagaries of economic fluctuations and technological disruptions.

As we gaze into the horizon unfolding before us, one thing is clear: in an AI-era, the knowledge you held at retirement entry might not be sufficient by the end. Hence, arming ourselves through lifelong learning and staying abreast of the AI-driven world's developments isn't just a survival strategy—it is your secret weapon to flourish in this new normal, particularly when it comes to retirement planning.

So, let the quest for learning be relentless. For amidst the constant evolution and inevitability of change, one's power to learn, adapt, and evolve is our most formidable defense.

**The symbiotic relationship between humans and AI**

We're standing at the precipice of a new era—an era where Artificial Intelligence (AI) isn't just a concept seen in sci-fi movies; It's our reality. The AI revolution is changing every facet of our lives, including our perceptions, preparations, and, indeed, the actuality of our retirements. Yet, it's paramount to grasp that AI is not a standalone entity but part of a complex relationship with human beings. Understanding this symbiotic relationship between humans and AI is crucial in the context of retirement planning amidst AI advancements.

First and foremost, we must staunchly erase the idea of 'us versus them'—the notion that AI and humans are in a race. Instead, we should focus on a theme which takes center stage in the context of AI and human interaction —that is 'us and them'. This means emphasizing the collaboration between humans and AI, recognizing that AI, in the end, is a tool crafted by us, for us.

This human-AI symbiosis can broadly be seen in two ways. First, AI can significantly enhance human capabilities in making financial or retirement decisions. It does this by analyzing vast amounts of data, identifying patterns, and providing insights that would otherwise be overwhelming or impossible for humans. In this way, AI becomes a powerful assistant, helping humans make more knowledgeable, data-driven decisions.

Secondly, it can free humans from mundane, repetitive tasks, consequently giving them more time to focus on creative, complex problem-solving tasks. For instance, in retirement planning, AI can automate many processes – calculating risks in potential investment opportunities, regularly balancing your retirement portfolio, or even predicting future income streams based on your financial habits.

Despite the awe-inspiring capabilities of AI, the human element retains its irreplaceable role – the human touch. In the process of retirement planning, while AI can process and furnish us with data-informed suggestions, the ultimate decision-making power is, and should be, in human hands. This makes the journey more personal and adaptable to each individual's unique needs, dreams, and situations.

The symbiotic human-AI relationship isn't without its risks and rewards. The risks include invasion of privacy, reliance on programming that could be wrong, algorithmic biases and the misuse of AI technology. However, the potential rewards cannot be understated - improved efficiency, enhanced decision-making abilities, more time, personalization, and significant technological advancements.

Considering all these, the way forward lies in understanding this transformative relationship between humans and AI—embracing AI for its potential to revolutionize traditional retirement plans, while recognizing and addressing its risks. We must work hand-in-hand with AI, harnessed by our value-based steering, to ensure it serves in our best interests. This relationships marks a journey of humans supplemented by AI in designing a more secure, efficient and personalized retirement plan, empowering us to better navigate the ever-changing tides of the future.

Encouraging communities to embrace and shape the AI-driven future

The tidal wave of artificial intelligence (AI) is undeniably sweeping across the globe, significantly altering aspects of human life and fundamentally transforming facets of societies. Perhaps one of the most crucial junctures of our time lies in the way communities respond to these sweeping changes, particularly in the arena of retirement planning and financial security. This paves the way for a two-pronged call to action — not just to embrace the advancements from the AI tide but also to become the shapers of our own AI-driven future.

For many, AI and its implications may seem overwhelming, or even intimidating, often leaving them feeling lost in a world that feels increasingly digitized and impersonal. However, it's crucial to dispel these notions, enabling communities to see AI as a beneficial tool rather than an alienating force.

The starting point in embracing AI lies in equipping ourselves with knowledge and understanding. This includes awareness about the latest AI-driven tools available for financial and retirement planning, the safety measures to ensure data privacy, overcoming the 'black box' problem, and the potential rewards and risks.

Furthermore, effective education initiatives from schools, community centers, and financial institutions can play a pivotal role in making AI less intimidating and more accessible.

Beyond embracing the AI present, it's equally important for communities to actively shape their AI-driven future. This means not just adapting to the changes thrust upon us, but also proactively influencing the development and direction of AI, especially in terms of ethical considerations and fairness.

Public discussions, open forums, and citizen assemblies should be convened on AI topics to ensure voices are heard-particularly those of seniors and retirees who may feel marginalized by the rapid tech advancements.

Policymakers need to step in here, to not only provide the necessary regulations around AI use but also to ensure transparency and to heed citizen voices in these policies. Regulations should ensure AI advancements do not overstep privacy boundaries and that AI serves the interests of all community members, not just a select few.

Bridging AI with community needs and values, thus shaping a future that is both technological but rooted in community spirit. Encouraging 'People-Powered AI' where communities collectively determine how AI is used and incorporated in their lives, particularly for retirement planning.

As we tread deeper into the AI era, it's crucial that we transition from passive observers to active participants. By fostering a collaborative, inclusive, and proactive approach, communities can form a new social contract with AI, making it a positive force in shaping a secure and equitable retirement future. The AI revolution isn't just about technological innovation. It's about using those innovations to build a future that resonates with our collective dreams, values, and aspirations.

Emphasizing the collective responsibility in shaping AI's role

The role of AI in the modern world isn't just a matter of technological progress. It's a significant societal issue with substantial implications for every aspect of human life, including retirement. As such, it necessitates collective responsibility in shaping AI's role in our world - because ensuring a secure and equitable future for all doesn't merely fall on the shoulders of AI developers, industry experts, or government officials. It falls on all of us.

Collective responsibility is predicated on acknowledging that decisions about AI utilization and implementation should not be determined by a select few but made collectively by all stakeholders - including average citizens, retirees, community leaders, educators, entrepreneurs, and policymakers. It involves fostering a democratic ethos where diverse voices are heard, considered, and prioritized.

Most importantly, collective responsibility recognizes that shaping AI's role isn't a one-off task, but an ongoing activity. It evolves as AI itself evolves and as societal values, needs, and understandings shift with time.

Each social actor brings to the fore unique perspectives and understandings that can guide the responsible usage and management of AI:

People on the fringes of technology - including the older generation planning their retirements - can help identify the potential pitfalls, biases, or ethical issues that tech insiders may overlook. They offer invaluable insights into making AI-driven retirement planning tools more user-friendly, accessible, and equitable.

AI developers and industry experts are not mere technological innovators; they are also social shapers. Their role extends beyond developing AI systems to ensuring these systems are transparent, accountable, and don't perpetuate systemic injustices or biases.

Policymakers are responsible for creating the necessary legal and regulatory frameworks that promote responsible AI usage. However, their role also lies in fostering a culture of AI literacy, ensuring that citizens can navigate, understand, and influence AI policies and decisions.

Lastly, educators are the indispensable bridges that help translate tech jargons into plain language, facilitating the general public's understanding of AI and the implications it harbors for their retirement planning.

In summary, emphasizing collective responsibility in shaping AI's role isn't about placing blame or burden on specific individuals or groups. Instead, it's about fostering a societal culture where decisions about AI are made collectively, considering the vast array of needs, perspectives, and values that characterize our diverse society.

As we chart the course into the AI-driven future, we must

remember that this navigational compass is a collective one. Every decision, every policy, every innovation impacts us all. It's not merely about crafting our retirement in the AI era. It's about crafting an era of AI that reflects the collective dreams, hopes, and shared values of retirees and everyone in between.

The fairness of AI pertains to its non-discriminative nature, ensuring that it doesn't perpetuate social biases or prejudices. Inclusivity, on the other hand, implies that AI is accessible and usable to all, irrespective of their socio-economic or educational backgrounds.

However, the concepts of fairness and inclusivity do not stop at the design or use of AI-based systems. It also relates to AI's implications and impacts. Are the insights derived from AI-based financial tools equally advantageous to all? Are the repercussions of AI-induced changes in the job market disproportionately harmful to certain sections of the society? Questions such as these underscore the need for championing fairness and inclusivity in the era of AI.

All societal actors, including AI developers, users, policymakers, educators, and retirees themselves, have a role to play in advocating for fairness and inclusivity in the AI scenario.

AI developers must ensure their creations are built and trained on impartial, representative data. Although achieving perfect fairness might not always be feasible, developers should strive, as much as possible, for transparency in how their algorithms function, and be willing to correct identified sources of bias.

Regular users, particularly retirees, play a pivotal role by holding companies accountable for their offering's fairness and inclusivity, promoting the specialization of AI tools catered to various user demographics.

Policymakers must enact legislation and regulations which ensure that the AI systems continue to promote fairness and inclusivity. This includes protecting against discriminatory algo-bias, ensuring citizens' digital literacy, thus encouraging broad-based AI access and participation.

The role of educators is imperative here. By making AI education not just a privilege for a select few but widely accessible, they help in democratizing the knowledge, making it inclusive to all.

AI shapes the landscapes of numerous aspects of human life, including our retirement. As such, its inclusivity and fairness, or the lack thereof, doesn't affect one section of the society but society at its whole.

The future we aim to construct isn't merely an AI-empowered world; it's an AI-empowered world characterized by inclusivity, fairness, and equality of opportunities and outcomes. Because a world where technology advances, but society regresses, is no advancement at all.

We stand on the brink of a new era, an era characterised by exponential technological advancements, wherein Artificial Intelligence (AI) will progressively shape aspects of human life in ways we can't fully predict. As AI permeates our retirement planning, our approach to this spectral reality must be proactive. A passive stance will leave us ill-prepared; rather, we must be refreshingly anticipatory and catalytic, fostering an ethical, secure future for all.

## Embracing Technology with a Vision

The first proactive step is cultivating a forward-thinking mindset. It's about embracing AI as not a villainous agent of unemployment and insecurity but as an enabler, a tool that could augment our capabilities, streamline our retirement planning and provide us with opportunities previously unheard of, if steered ethically.

This begins with fostering AI literacy. In an AI-dominant world, understanding AI and its implications is not a luxury, but a necessity, equivalent to reading and writing in today's world. We should aim at adopting AI education and awareness campaigns, workshops for elderly, and integrating AI curriculums in schools and universities.

## Staying Ahead of The Curve

As the implications of AI are vast and evolving, lifelong learning becomes crucial. We need a shift from thinking about education as a preparatory stage for our jobs to one that continues throughout life. AI-based courses, webinars and skilling programs can help us stay relevant, adapt to changing job market dynamics, and secure our retirement in the age of AI.

It's not just about preparing ourselves to live in an AI-empowered world, but about shaping it. This requires understanding the ethical implications of AI (like privacy issues, algo-bias), staying informed about regional and global AI policy debates, and voicing our opinions, thereby, playing a role in the evolution of ethical AI norms and legislations.

## Advocating for Inclusive, Ethical AI

Additionally, we have the democratic responsibility of advocating for a fair, inclusive AI ecosystem. We need to push for governmental and organisational policies that prohibit discriminatory AI practices, promote transparency in AI operations, and ensure an equitable distribution of AI's benefits.

The proactive steps to secure an ethical future are not confined to individual capacities alone. They extend to urging finance corporations to adopt AI whilst prioritizing data protection, urging tech companies to make their AI systems as transparent as possible, and urging policymakers to prioritize ethical considerations in their AI strategy.

**Harnessing the Power of Collective Action**

Technology has the potential to either divide or unite; it’s our actions that determine its course. The impact of any individual effort might seem infinitesimal, but a collective endeavour can overcome any hurdle. Joining hands with communities, organizations and forums advocating for ethical use of AI can amplify our voices and bring substantive changes.

Navigating this era of AI may seem daunting, but it's through proactive measures and continuous learning that we can guide the tides of change to our advantage. Our future is a canvas, AI is but a palette of colours; it's upon us to paint a picture of ethical, secure retirement, for ourselves and for generations to come.

This chapter ends here, but our journey into the era of AI has just begun – a journey of continuous learning, adaptation, preparation, and proactive measures. As we sail forward, let our lodestar be not fear but ambition, not uncertainty but eagerness, brimming with the conviction that a secure, ethical future in the era of AI is not just a possibility but a reality within our reach.

Printed in Great Britain
by Amazon

6beaa138-752e-4480-813e-afffe747e715R01